Praise for

# THE ENERGY ADVANTAGE

"Ricardo Sunderland knows what it means to think, live, and work holistically. In *The Energy Advantage*, he masterfully breaks down what it takes to harness your energy and take actionable steps toward unleashing your full potential as a leader. And I can tell you from personal experience, his guidance is best in class."

—Jane Fraser, CEO of Citigroup

"Ricardo Sunderland was able to help me realize that leadership is not a burden but a privilege. To enjoy the privilege takes ENERGY. Ricardo's ability to unlock full energy is his gift to others."

—Alan Jope, former CEO of Unilever

"In a truly compassionate and authentic fashion, Ricardo Sunderland reveals the keys for a profound journey of personal transformation through our own energy. Incredibly powerful!"

—Alejandro Reynal, CEO of Four Seasons

"Ricardo Sunderland's framework allows you to cut through the noise and make the right decisions."

—DJ Patil, former US Chief Data Scientist

"Ricardo Sunderland's approach on energy has helped me solve how to do more with less and, despite the burden, how to enjoy my role more."

—Hector Grisi Checa, CEO of Grupo Santander

"Ricardo Sunderland's book makes a passionate and compelling plea: Unleashing your energy starts with shifting the energy within you. By connecting to your deeper source, you can unleash your full creative potential."
—Dolf van den Brink, CEO and Chairman of the Executive
Board of Heineken

"Life-changing. Finding deeper ways to connect with my own energy changes the energy I project and amplifies the positive impact I have."
—Judith Hartmann, former Deputy CEO
and CFO of ENGIE

"We need more thought leaders to be themselves both in their professional and their personal lives. Ricardo Sunderland's approach to an energy mindset shift can become a true positive force in the world of business."
—Daniel Servitje Montull, Chairman
and CEO of Grupo Bimbo

"True leadership means being your true self—all in. Ricardo Sunderland's insights should be a go-to for all aspiring leaders."
—Nicolas Aguzin, CEO of Hong Kong Stock Exchange

# THE
# ENERGY
# ADVANTAGE

THE
# ENERGY
# ADVANTAGE

*How to Go from Managing Your Time
to Mastering Your Energy*

# RICARDO
# SUNDERLAND

HarperCollins
LEADERSHIP

AN IMPRINT OF HARPERCOLLINS

ISBN 978-1-4002-4892-6 (eBook)
ISBN 978-1-4002-4891-9 (HC)

Library of Congress Control Number: 2023952312

Printed in the United States of America

24 25 26 27 28  LBC  5 4 3 2 1

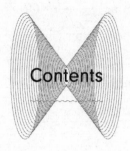

# Contents

# Contents

TO PATY, DIANA, RICKY, AND ANDY—

thank you for always challenging,
inspiring, and sustaining me.

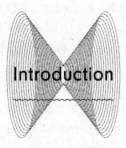

# Introduction

In September 2020, Citigroup announced that, the following February, Jane Fraser would become the company's CEO, making her the first woman to break Wall Street's glass ceiling. I had been coaching Jane since 2015, when she took the role of CEO of Latin America at Citigroup, so when we met a few weeks after the announcement of her new role I asked her if there was any sage advice from the many CEOs, heads of state, and friends who had called to congratulate her that we should work into her development plan.

"I've gotten a lot of advice that I need to take to heart," she said, "and one comment that's really sticking with me came from Ernesto Zedillo." I knew that Zedillo—a Citigroup board member and the former president of Mexico—was a wise person whom Jane respected. "He said, 'Jane, as CEO, your real challenge isn't to manage your time but to manage your energy. If you succeed at that, you'll get everything done that you need to get done, and you'll be fulfilled while doing so. And that in turn will make you a great resource for the company.'"

Hearing that from Jane was a gratifying moment. It confirmed what Jane and I had been working on for some time and what I hear consistently from many of my clients. Consider

Dolf van den Brink, who became CEO of Heineken, in June 2020, just as the full force of the COVID-19 pandemic was sweeping around the globe. He and I had been working together before that, so I had an inside perspective on the unfolding crisis, and I can say confidently that the enormity of that challenge can't be overstated. Not only did Dolf have to take up the reins on a vast consumer business, but he had to do so at a time when most consumers weren't able to go to bars and restaurants in person. Sales plunged, and the company simply withdrew its guidance for investors for the entire year. No one was yet sure where the bottom might be found.

Two years later, Heineken had not only survived but was in the midst of a deep transformation project called EverGreen. Of course, the retreat of COVID helped. But when I asked Dolf what else contributed, he said:

"It was a combination of things, for sure. I already deeply believed that leadership is about marshaling and unleashing the energies of the organization. But the crucible of the crisis helped me realize that this starts by marshaling and unleashing the energies from within. From within your top leadership team and ultimately from within yourself. While our world was 'on fire' we actually connected more deeply with each other by also connecting more deeply with ourselves. It unleashed our full humanity and ultimately the creative force of the team and the organization."

That was another gratifying moment. Almost 100 percent of the leaders I work with begin by telling me that they have no time. The goal of my work is to help shift their mindset from *managing their time* to *mastering their energy*. Indeed, my life's purpose is to help leaders with impact *connect to and manage their energy to become humane leaders.*

The energy I discuss in this book—which I refer to as *intentional*—underlies our creativity and ability to impact others. When we have unconscious, mixed, or opposing intentions, we fight against ourselves and disrupt the creative process. When we learn to align our intentions—within ourselves and with the immediate group of people with whom we work—we tap into tremendous creativity.

So that's my goal in this book: to help you—whether you are a current or aspiring leader—make a shift that will be the key to your success. While most of the examples in the pages ahead are from my work with senior leaders, those clients routinely ask me, "Where were you fifteen years ago?" In other words, as they saw it, I could have been helpful, maybe even more helpful, at earlier stages in their careers.

Over the decade and a half that I've been doing this, I've identified a set of patterns that cut across cultures, industries, and organizational types. On the positive side, I kept coming across talented executives with a strong desire to grow and succeed, who drew upon their deep reserves of smarts, ambition, and curiosity to do so. But I also kept encountering a complex constellation of emotions that were holding many of these talented and ambitious people back professionally and reducing their ability to enjoy life. Stated simply, these highly accomplished executives were beset by self-limiting unconscious beliefs and fears. They were unhappy, and—when they finally got around to admitting it—they struggled with different levels of insecurity. They lived lives of intense and false emotional compartmentalization: for example, trying to be one person in the corner office (invincible warrior) and another person at the dinner table (sensitive spouse) and trying not to let those two lives bleed together and contradict each other.

But that approach to life can't work. And even if it could, it would be limiting for both those leaders and the organization that they lead. Why? Because that struggle consumes a great deal of energy, the management of which is the central focus of this book. And at the same time, what's needed in the corporate world today is *humane leaders*—people at all levels in an organization whose heads, hearts, and creative power are in coherence with their true selves.

Stated somewhat differently, humane leadership can come only from people whose personal and professional worlds are integrated in a seamless way. It can come only from people who have easy access to both the left (rational) and right (emotional) sides of their brains. It can come only from people who are comfortable being their true selves—anytime, anywhere.

I help my clients embark on a life-changing journey. Given how different we all are as individuals, it won't surprise you to learn that every one of those journeys is different, especially when it comes to the "how." One size does not fit all. That said, there is a crucial common element across all my clients: *they are all human beings,* and they all share the same energy and its potential. Conceptions of human energy differ widely, especially between Eastern and Western cultures. Yes, there's a gulf there, but experience tells me that it's not a chasm. There *are* commonalities. I hope that one of this book's contributions will be to serve as a bridge between Eastern and Western conceptions of human energy.

I have found it helpful to think of our human energy field, or HEF, expressing itself in seven levels, each associated with a different type of life experience.[1] The first four make up our physical, emotional, and mental energy, and the last three involve our spiritual energy. Researchers have reported measuring different frequencies at each of the levels of the HEF—in other words, forces that are invisible to the naked eye but exert powerful influences.

So perhaps you're now asking a good and obvious question: "Ricardo, are you saying that we're going to manage our energy by focusing on things we can't touch or see?" My answer is yes. We can't see electricity, and yet we manage that expertly in our everyday lives, right? And we can't see emotions, but they certainly come to bear directly on our levels of happiness and success. Ultimately, we have to look at the *outcomes* and go with that flow.

If you want to learn how to manage your energy, you can choose to do so on these seven levels. Note the word *choose*. How deeply you want to get into this is truly your choice. As I'll explain, you'll have to start with the physical, emotional, and mental levels and—if you choose—work your way into the spiritual levels.

It's a bit like being a runner. Jogging requires one kind of commitment. A 10K race requires another. A marathon requires yet another. No, marathoners are not more virtuous than joggers, but they've made a deeper commitment—and they can expect to be rewarded for that extra investment in their discipline.

What does all of this have to do with leaders? Leaders who understand how to set their agendas and intention based on managing their energy ultimately achieve enhanced levels of freedom of choice. They have the blessing of peace of mind. They experience *joy*. They become a bigger and better version of themselves—they and the teams and organizations they lead achieve the energy advantage.

When meeting for the first time, many of my clients caution me that they've already had their fill of executive coaches. But I've learned to expect that reaction, so I rarely refer to myself in those terms. If pressed, I might call myself an adviser, or even a transformational coach. I like the way one of my clients recently put it: Ricardo teaches you to self-coach. But the learning goes both ways, and I want to share not only what I teach my clients but also what I've learned from them.

Most of my clients, at least in the early stages of our relationships, roll their eyes and let me know that they're turned off by words like *humane leadership*. They tend to dismiss such ideas as fanciful, soft, or self-indulgent: not the stuff of "real" business. They worry aloud that a "humane leader" sounds like it might be too personal and probably irrelevant to making the business grow and making it more profitable. In fact, as we will see, following the path to humane leadership is very *good* business. Organizations that invest in helping their leaders do so tend to thrive.

I rarely argue with my clients—at least early on in our relationships. Instead, I meet them where they are, and we proceed from there. I get them to tell me what's bugging them, and sooner or later, they open up to me. They all say, in so many words, that they want to remember the joy they felt back when they were in their twenties, when they felt less burdened, felt *freer*, felt like they had more and better choices, and felt like they had more time to themselves. (Does this sound familiar?) They look back to a time, maybe not so many years earlier, when they were more inspirational as a leader—and wish they could get back to generating that kind of inspiration and excitement. They are tired, but they have trouble sleeping. They are lonely and feel estranged from both their work colleagues and their families. Some are concerned that when they are challenged in the workplace, they overreact, get overwhelmed, and turn into intellectual bullies. Some are convinced that they are impostors—frauds who are going to be caught out and sent packing. And many believe that, one way or another, sooner or later, they're going to fail.

Many of them feel that as you move up the organizational ladder, the demands of the job become so intense that *you don't belong to yourself anymore*—a phrase that came up unprompted many times in our firm's recent CEO survey[2]—and many of these extraordinary individuals fear that they may not be up to the job. "Leadership is increasingly about humanity, sharing imperfection, being authentic and empathetic," one respondent wrote. In addition to winning the minds of the people around you, you also need to win their hearts. This is no small feat—and as you ascend the hierarchy, your own changing role greatly increases this challenge. As Harvard Business School professor Linda A. Hill states in her compelling book *Collective Genius*, "Simply setting direction no longer works; you need to co-create with your teams in new ways, you need to shape context."[3]

That phrase, *shape context,* stuck with me, and I used it in a workshop that I ran a few years back. That workshop was attended by Jane Fraser, who was then Citigroup's CEO of Latin America. I noticed that Jane was taking copious notes while I was talking, and a little later in the session I asked her what she had been writing down. "I've been trying to find a phrase, and a philosophy, that distills the essence of the type of leader I want to become," she replied. "I think I just heard it: being a leader who *shapes context*, rather than direction."

The path to effectively shaping context—the path to *leadership*—lies in mastering your energy. For most people, this means shifting your energy in ways that will help you manage it more effectively. *That's the core premise of this book*. If you manage your energy effectively, your time will seem to expand, almost magically, along with your clarity of thought and creative power.

As I've mentioned, close to 100 percent of the leaders I work with begin their journey by telling me that they have no time. When I ask them why that's the case, I get back a thousand different explanations, some of which may be familiar to you. "This job is enormous," I hear. "I have to prove myself. The company's in a crisis. I don't trust my team and have to rebuild it." Or, "I have a great team that I have to challenge and retain. This recession is driving us into the ground. Global supply chains have collapsed." And so on, and so on.

"What's holding you back?" I ask. "What's keeping you from connecting to your source of energy?" Because no matter what that real-world challenge is, *freeing up more minutes to deal with it isn't the answer.* Even if you succeed by throwing additional minutes at it, the next energy-draining challenge is going to come down the road, and sooner or later you will surely run out of minutes to squeeze out of your day.

So managing your energy sets you up for success and a fulfilling life. Conversely, *not* doing so limits your ability to assess the opportunities that come your way. Choices that should be easy to make become unnecessarily murky and complex—and chew up a lot of time that should be going elsewhere.

At the start of every engagement, I ask my clients to imagine having a magic wand: After our last session, where would they like to end up after learning how to manage their energy? Setting forth without a sense of direction would be a waste of energy. Setting forth with a clear intention—think of it as a North Star—is essential to the success of the work.

I don't present myself as an expert in this field, and I'm quick to say that very little of the material in these pages is entirely original to me. I'm more of a lamplighter than a trailblazer. But I bring together a combination of disciplines and alternative (and sometimes disruptive!) practices that I've experienced firsthand, with the goal of helping very successful people be and become the fuller versions of the self to which they aspire.

I was also *not* alone in my journey. I had wise teachers, and here I want to honor Erica Ariel Fox, Ester Martinez, Albert Goslan, Dick Schwartz, Lynda Caesara, and Scott Coady, with deep gratitude. A very special bow of appreciation to Amy Elizabeth Fox[4] and Jill Ader, who have been the connective energy behind it all.

My journey so far has given me immense joy, and I am looking forward to sharing that immense joy with you.

# Part I

# Energy

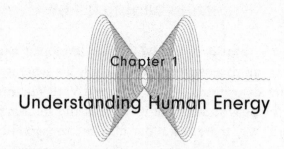

## Chapter 1

# Understanding Human Energy

When was the last time you had a little kid in the house?

Especially in the early morning, it's humbling. The parents and grandparents, reaching for that second cup of coffee, are still bleary eyed and moving slowly. Maybe they exchange a few short sentences about how they really need to *get on a better schedule, get some more sleep*, and so on.

Meanwhile, that toddler hasn't stopped running since his little feet hit the ground. Of course, coffee isn't yet on his menu, and so far this morning he hasn't gotten into anything sugary. And yet, he's *tearing the place up*—building up this, knocking down that, eavesdropping on the conversations around him and chiming in randomly, disappearing around one corner at high speed only to reappear around another corner, barely stopping to catch his breath, and pretty jazzed about the whole experience of life.

It's a humbling, exhausting, and inspiring spectacle, all at once.

And yet, it's our natural state. This is how we come into this world—with our hearts so full of energy and our young minds so empty and eager to take in all that life has to offer.

## THINKING ABOUT ENERGY

In the past several decades, we in the developed world have become a lot more sensitive to energy: how it's generated, transmitted, and distributed. We've wrestled with nuclear power, fracking, the pros and cons of windmills and solar arrays, and much more. We've argued about how far conservation (as an alternative to new power-generation capacity) can take us. The most recent debates about energy have focused on storage, and the relatively rapid advent of electric vehicles has sharpened these questions. An electric car needs batteries. Well, what are these batteries made of? (Where's all that lithium going to come from?) Are they recyclable? How far can you travel on a charge? Where can you get your batteries recharged and how long does it take?

One day several years back, it struck me that we, ourselves, are a kind of electric vehicle. Over time I teased out this metaphor further, deciding that we're actually some sort of hybrid, in terms of energy. We consume food: our equivalent of the fossil fuels that we put into our internal-combustion vehicle or the electric current that people put into the batteries of their electric cars. We burn that food to move our muscles and exercise our brains. If we take in too much fuel and fail to burn off that potential energy, we store it. (We get larger.)

But at the same time, we're deriving stimulation from the people and circumstances around us: a different kind of energy. People take and give energy in different ways. Some people thrive when they're immersed in this kind of energy; others— the introverts among us—tend to feel more energized when they withdraw. But looking back to the larger point, we humans are some sort of hybrid.

But along comes that little kid who challenges my somewhat shaky metaphor. That toddler isn't just feeding back the energy that his doting family provides. I don't think the

Tuesday morning whirlwind is just a reflection of Monday night's dinner. And he's certainly not soaking up energy from those slow-moving older generations. No, something else is going on. The toddler is tapping into an inner energy source. Let's call it *human energy*.

How do we get access to it—and why does that matter?

## THE ENERGY WITHIN

I am a great fan of the work of the late Barbara Ann Brennan. Barbara Ann Brennan was a former NASA research scientist who transformed herself—somewhat reluctantly, at the beginning of her journey—into a human energy expert. It took her many years to make that transition, but over time, she brought her two seemingly different backgrounds to bear on her work in ways that are both fascinating and useful.

Her books focus on what she called the "human energy field"—mentioned in my introduction—and how people can use this field to improve their health in a holistic way. I think of her work as a sort of medicine that was intended for one specific use but which soon proved to be therapeutic in other applications—some of which inspired me to evolve my coaching practice. These uses show up at various points along the way in this book.

Brennan contextualized the role of energy in our lives. She wrote about mastering the human energy flow *outward*—from one human to another and from one human to the world. In her distinctive voice, at once lyrical and a little stilted, she described the joy that arises out of that mastery and the benefits that accrue to the person who achieves that mastery:

> Most likely, as a child, in a very natural unplanned way, you let yourself go fully into whatever was at hand.

That is what you still do, in those wonderful moments of creative abandon when you have given over to the life energy that flows out of you from an internal source. Then the colors are brighter, the tastes sweeter, the air more fragrant, and sounds around you create a symphony. You are not the exception; everyone has these experiences.[1]

I became hung up on one of those phrases, the first time I read it: *the life energy that flows out of you from an internal source.* I searched in vain for a concise definition of what Brennan was talking about there, even though I felt instinctively that I knew what she meant. No such luck. So, with apologies in advance to Brennan, let me define human energy, at least in a way that serves our purposes in this book. *Human energy is the creative power within all of us.* It's the driving force that creates and animates all of the powerful experiences of our lives.

This is actually an ancient idea. As Aristotle put it, "The energy of the mind is the essence of life." Sometimes that energy becomes evident and accessible through individual experiences. For example, think about how you feel when you're watching a breathtaking sunset. Think about where your favorite song takes you, once you let go and really *listen* to it, truly connecting with it. But more often in today's complex society, it is manifested in our interactions with other people.

As you can see, we're getting further and further away from my metaphorical battery. Think again of that little kid, tapping into an energy that *flows out of him from an internal source.* It's as if he has his own little power plant, somewhere within, with its own magical, inexhaustible fuel supply. And—this turns out to be very important—*he's able to tap into it at will.*

Meanwhile, the adults around him don't have anything like the same sparkle. Why not? Did our fuel supply from our childhood, supposedly inexhaustible, run out? Or have we simply lost easy access to the energy it generates?

I'm convinced it's the latter.

## ENERGY BLOCKERS AND ENERGY GIVERS

For most of us—probably even all of us—something unexpected and unwelcome happened during our early childhood. Everyone's version of this experience is different in its details, but for many of us, it was manifested as some sort of unmet need. Maybe we didn't get as much love as we needed. Maybe we earned attention, appreciation, and affection only when we *achieved* something. The result, in all cases, was that we experienced emotional pain.

Naturally enough, we reacted to this pain by trying to stop it and get what we needed. How? By developing strategies to protect ourselves from these hurtful emotions and by changing how we interacted with those around us. Slowly but surely, we developed a new "emotional pattern"—a concept I'll return to later in the chapter. For now, let's just think of it as our personality. We created new personalities for ourselves, and, in one sense, it *worked*. We got more of what we needed to feel safe again.

But on a more fundamental level, it *didn't* work. Developing an emotional pattern moves us away from who we really are. It moves us away from accessing our human energy—that energy that so astonishes us in a toddler.

So how is this emotional pattern created? Think of it as an emotional balancing system within us. When our needs went unmet again and again, we experienced pain, in the form of sadness or anger or heartbreak. Well, we can't stay in pain indefinitely, so at some point, our balancing system kicked in. It helped us create unconscious protective strategies that we applied again and again, successfully, to get us back to feeling safe and out of pain. Ultimately, these strategies become part of our personality—part of who we believe we are.

I picked those words carefully—"who we believe we are." These emotional balancing strategies work well, for the time being—but later in life, when the complexity of things begins to overwhelm us, they can start to hold us back and create unintended consequences.

Like what? Have you ever snapped at someone, stormed out the door, and—once you were alone—experienced a wave of guilt and asked yourself, *Why did I react this way, again? That person didn't deserve all that!* When we feel overwhelmed, *fear* takes hold of us. It's at these moments that our balancing system shows up again to support us, reinforcing our emotional pattern, helping us avoid that original pain. But in the process, a new energy loop is created—a sort of short circuit, if you will, sparked by fear. And from that time forward, fear activates that short circuit. When we are afraid, we become disconnected from our center—from our human energy—and we gradually forget who we really are.

This sequence is important in my work, and it's important to the arguments I make in this book. We need to understand where that pain we encountered at a young age has led us. We need to understand the central role that fear played in the development of our emotional pattern and in our search for ways to protect ourselves. It's a key topic, and I'll return to it in chapter 2.

## THE EMOTIONAL PATTERN

When you're born, you're born in pure bliss, right? Your heart is full and your mind is empty. You are a sponge. You start to connect with things and make sense out of life, rationally and emotionally. And then something happens—as discussed above—and you get hurt. This is the root of the emotional pattern.

In many cases, that hurt is an unmet need. For example, the infant Me needs to be fed, and so I make "feed-me" noises. But suppose my parents have joined the "let them cry it out" school of child-rearing: "If we keep feeding this guy, we're never going to get to sleep. Let's just let him cry until he understands that he'll get fed in the morning, when we wake up." Right? Well, no, according to most experts.[2] But let's move ahead with the scenario. So I cry and I don't eat, and I cry and I don't eat, then I suddenly realize that when I stop crying for a longer period of time, I get fed. So I stop crying, and I get fed, and I stop crying, and I get fed. There's a part of me that starts to realize, "If I show an emotion—or if I ask in this unacceptable way to be fed—I'm not going to get fed."

That hurt starts to create a mindset that says that *emotions won't get you what you want*. What we do next is look for ways to protect ourselves. Because of fear, we start losing access to our human energy, and we start projecting fear (and the emotions that result from being in fear) outward into the world. As we grow and express these protective emotions—collectively, our emotional pattern—we become masters at masking our own emotions. In our professional lives, we create a shield: defensive armor to fend off what we perceive to be a hostile and dangerous world. We're precluded from speaking and following our own truth. *Professionalism* means acting in ways that take us away from our original personality, from our humanity, and therefore block access to energy.

Ultimately, the challenge becomes one of stepping out of that emotional pattern and tapping into that human energy source—the same one that you knew briefly, so long ago.

One of my clients, whom I'll call Louise, experienced a great deal of development trauma in her upbringing. She had no idea, until well along in our journey together, how much her early reactions to that trauma were still with her in the present—holding her back, forcing her to shift her energy in what I'd call an attacking energy or a perpetrator energy. Her teams were constantly experiencing her leadership style as an attack. And like a dog with a bone, she stayed in fight mode just for the sake of fighting.

Louise was horrified to learn about this perception. She had recently earned the CEO's job. She had always won the *minds* of the people around her—she was brilliant, in her attacks— but now she felt like she had to start winning their hearts, and it seemed like a hopeless quest.

I assured her it wasn't. What she had to do, I said, was step out of this constraining, confining emotional pattern in which she had been trapped all those years ago and get back to being her true self. It certainly wasn't easy to resolve—especially because she was highly successful, and she was convinced that her personality had helped her win the corner office.

I'm happy to report that in relatively short order, she was able to not just understand where her negative energy was coming from but to feel it, acknowledge it, and shift it. Today, there's a near total congruence between what she says and how she wants to conduct herself—that is, *acting* on what she says. She has gone from being an attacker to an inspiring leader. Before you can transform your personality to incorporate the set of behaviors you want to embrace, you must first shift your energy.

That can't happen until you're ready and able to unlock your emotional pattern. Easier said than done—but still doable. In later chapters, I'll describe in greater detail how to change these ingrained personality traits and shift your personality back to where it was originally, and where you would like it to be.

## SPIRITUAL ENERGY

Let's talk about woo woo.

*Woo woo* can be defined as unconventional beliefs regarded as having little or no scientific basis, especially those relating to spirituality, mysticism, or alternative medicine. Sometimes I invoke this term to rein myself in, as in, *Hey, Ricardo: enough with the woo woo; you are losing them; get back down to earth.* By and large, my clients enjoy it when I say stuff like that in their presence.

Given the fact that in this chapter we are considering human energy and the paths to accessing it, we must look beyond the physical, emotional, and mental to the fourth bucket: *spiritual* energy. So let's get the idea of spirituality squarely on the table. I'll offer my own definition: *spirituality is the journey toward connecting back with our original bliss—our original human energy.* Note that I didn't say the *destination* of the journey, although it can be that as well. But mainly, spirituality is an unfolding process: a journey rather than an end point.

Some very down-to-earth people have engaged with, and even endorsed, explorations in the spiritual dimension. I'm thinking, for example, of the late Elisabeth Kübler-Ross: psychiatrist, hospice pioneer, and author of the 1969 international best-seller *On Death and Dying*, in which she introduced her "five stages of grief" model. Elisabeth Kübler-Ross contributed a blurb for Barbara Ann Brennan's first book, *Hands of Light*, which she described as "a delight for an open-minded person who is willing to look beyond the 'real' of our present-day understanding and knowledge."[3]

I'll pick out just a few of Kübler-Ross's words and scramble them up for my own purposes. Although many, if not most, of my clients resist the idea that we might be venturing into the realm of the spiritual on our journey, in fact we are. I think there *is* delight to be found on that journey—which goes beyond our present-day understanding—but only if the traveler is open-minded enough.

And as you've probably anticipated, "delight" translates into joy, and joy into energy. In William Blake's words: "Energy is the only life, and is from the body; and reason is the bound or outward circumference of energy. Energy is eternal delight."[4]

Energy is from the body and is eternal delight. Well stated, William.

You connect to spiritual energy by surrendering to the mystery of life. And this is a highly practical goal to embrace, because embracing the mystery of life can unlock immense energy within us.

Conversely, failing to embrace that mystery tends to drain us. For example, many of the leaders I work with—even some of the most successful CEOs—regularly ask themselves, *Why me? There were many others more capable than me, more connected than me, more resourceful than me, more deserving than me.* These kinds of questions literally haunt them. Even after they've reached the top of the house, they absolutely don't believe that they deserve to be there. As a result, they expend far too much energy and time trying to prove to others that they are not a fake.

When I encounter the "why me" question—which absolutely comes up in far more corner offices than most people would imagine—I sometimes suggest an alternative question: *Who am I to ask, "Why me?"*

Not everybody gets my point right off the bat—but ultimately, they all do. I'm saying, without using exactly these words, that they have to surrender to the mystery of life. And guess what? When they do so, many of them, to their great surprise, *move forward.* Figuring out who you are, and *acting* on that understanding, is truly liberating. It's a huge weight off your shoulders. Being a spiritual being gives you faith.

Please note that I'm not saying this in a religious context. Figuring out who you are gives you faith in yourself, hope for the world—and a clearer path ahead.

## A STEP FURTHER

We've taken this somewhat winding road through the human-energy field, and means of access to it, because human energy is a core concept in my work. It serves as that gateway I've referred to: between Eastern philosophies and Western culture. Mastering human energy enables a leader to develop into a *humane* leader.

The journey toward the true version of yourself largely focuses on *getting access to your energy*—on multiple levels—and thereby managing your energy and gaining control of your life. Most people get this backward. They think that if only they can get control of their life, by which they mean their *time*, things will shake out in the right ways. But this is wrong and only leads to frustration—to more energy wasted.

At the beginning of this chapter, I sketched out a little slice of the reality of life with a two-year-old. If you could capture that reality on film, it would show a huge bundle of energy bouncing off all the low-energy adults in the room. That young child is totally tapped into his human energy; he hasn't yet encountered the myriad things that will start to block that energy.

Is this important? Yes. Most of us with dreams and ambitions understand that we need to be creative to succeed—in business, as in every other aspect of our lives. Here's a key takeaway: *your creative power reflects your energy level.* When properly balanced, your human energy can serve you and your creativity as an almost unlimited resource.

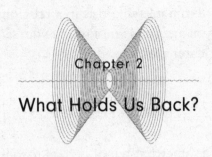

## Chapter 2

# What Holds Us Back?

If we can agree that gaining energy elevates us and having energy blocked brings us down, why don't we just go for the high as much as we can? Why do we allow ourselves to get sucked into the low far more often than we're even aware of?

The answer lies in a psychological phenomenon that I refer to as the *self-hijack*. Most of us assert that we want freedom of choice. We want to be the masters of our own fates. We want to chart our own course. We want to write our own story. Pick your favorite metaphor; there are many to choose from.

And yet, the truth is that we rarely enjoy that kind of freedom or lead that kind of self-realized life. We fall victim to self-hijacking. How? We lose control of our emotions, of ourselves. And when we do, we let other people write our story for us.

### THE SELF-HIJACK

I have a friend who on more than one occasion has claimed that he can't remember the last time he felt true joy. This almost always earns him a chorus of hoots and jeers, and so he stops talking about it. Until the next time, anyway.

I never join in the chorus. In fact, I feel very close to him, and protective of him, when he shows his vulnerability. Why? Because I have a personal story in the same vein. Somewhere around month six of my gestation within my mother's womb, her doctors decided that the pregnancy was at risk. My mother had to lie in bed for her entire third trimester, fearing the whole time that she would lose her first child. And down there in the uterus, I lost my urge to emerge. In a preverbal sort of way, I changed my mind.

I was born right on schedule, nine months on, seemingly happy and healthy. But I believe that the unending, clenching fear that my mother felt, in her final three months—often alone, not being allowed to move more than the bare minimum—fully imprinted itself on me. I emerged as a fearful little thing. I probably wasn't any needier than any other infant, but I believe I *felt* needier.

Now comes another twist in the story. Although my mother is in many ways a remarkable woman with a beautiful soul, as an emotionally needy child I demanded more attention from her than she was able to provide. That "attention gap" grew when my brother was born and got even worse when my parents left on a three-month holiday when I was three years old. I remember feeling thoroughly abandoned. At some point in there, I developed a stutter (which I ultimately overcame). All that said, I don't blame my parents for anything. I believe that they both loved me the best they could and found their role as parents satisfying. In fact, my mother recently told me that the experience of having and raising my brothers and me completely fulfilled her.

Meanwhile, though, the little boy who was me clearly needed more love than he was able to get at home. This was no one's fault; it's just the way it was. But in those critical formative years, my emotional balancing system created a part of me whose strategy was to please people as a way to earn their approval and love. I tried to please my mother and grandmother. I tried to please my father. I tried to please *everyone*.

I was relentless in applying that strategy—again and again and again. The more I helped and pleased people, the more positive response I got back, until it became a core part of me, of my personality: "Ricardo—always such a good kid!" It fueled itself, creating in me the need to *not let people down*, to *belong*. And although I have done deep personal work to get to a state of emotional self-acceptance, and to be free from the influence of this and other potential hurts, there is still some of this people-pleaser in me.

In a very real sense, I was self-hijacked—and every once in a while, I can still get self-hijacked.

Is that story from my childhood unique? Not really. The bare essentials of my early childhood overlap a great deal with the childhood stories of many very successful people, including many of my clients. These stories are the roots of what later in life become our fears and our self-limiting belief systems. Many of these roots are hidden in our unconscious. In our journeys toward becoming a humane leader, my clients seek them out, work on them, and search for healing paths. When they find them, they unlock immense energy and find additional freedom of choice.

## FEARS AND BELIEFS

What's at work in our life story—and again, this is the rule, rather than the exception—is what I call the *fear system*. We're afraid of some bad outcome, even if the trigger is only remotely related to the potential bad outcome. In my native Mexico we have a saying: "If you once get burned by milk, then you'll cry when you see a cow."

When our coping strategies appear to be at risk of failing, *fear* kicks in. We feel ourselves getting overwhelmed, and we revert to patterns of behavior that we hope will fend off that bad outcome. This isn't necessarily a conscious process; in fact, it's generally not—and the subterranean nature of this stuff complicates things. I'm acting this way (relentlessly!) even though I'm not sure *why* I'm acting this way.

The other ingredient in this mix is what I called the *belief system.* These beliefs can also govern us on both the conscious and unconscious levels. *Here's what I see when I look in the mirror. Here's what I believe about who I am and who I am not. . . . I am an introvert, I am an extrovert, I am not creative, vulnerability is weakness, I never bring work issues home and vice versa,* and so on.

If you are an adult, you are at this point in your life already pretty much hijacked. You're relying on coping strategies—your fear system—that were developed long ago by a young child, most likely under the age of seven or eight.[1] In addition, you're carrying around a view of yourself (your belief system) that almost certainly includes some self-limiting beliefs, which can present a distorted reality.

Now picture your own world. With each promotion, you put a little (or a lot!) more pressure on yourself. Having assessed the costs and the benefits of climbing the ladder—and of course based on your very real smarts and talents—you purposefully change your world. And by so doing, you set up a dynamic in which your unchanging coping strategies become less and less effective. Your belief system starts to seem more and more at odds with what you now see in the mirror, with what seems to be going on around you, and with what the world now seems to be demanding of you.

In the intimacy of our conversations, as the demands upon my clients start to overwhelm them, they begin to tell me about the boulder on their shoulders, the void in their stomachs, and the annoying voices in their heads.

## THE VOICES IN OUR HEADS

How do we know when we've been self-hijacked?

There are a number of telltale signs. One is that the voices in our head start to become louder and in extreme cases become difficult to live with.

Voices in our head?

I think you know what I'm talking about. Are you hearing a voice inside your head right now? A voice saying, *What is this guy talking about? I don't hear that voice!* Yes? Hear it? That's the voice I'm talking about.

I first learned about these voices from my sage friend Erica Ariel Fox, whose best-selling book *Winning from Within* introduced a transformative idea into the world of leadership development. Curious people are endlessly assessing what's going on around them—sometimes to learn about something new, sometimes to figure out whether a past lesson applies to a new situation, and sometimes simply because figuring out the world is fun. Well, that process of exploration tends to involve an internal dialogue, on a more or less conscious level. We talk to ourselves. You talk to yourself. It's a way of taking notes and locking down that new learning.

But sometimes Yourself talks back in unexpected ways and in unhelpful voices. One of these voices is that of the Critic. This voice looks over your shoulder, perhaps attempting to steer you and—over time—maybe even criticizing your every move. It often starts out as a reasonably friendly voice, something like a favorite uncle or a friend, but as your coping systems start to fold under pressure, the Critic becomes harsher, more demanding, even relentless. It takes over the internal dialogue, and your head gets filled up with your faults and doubts. The Critic stops simply being an observer; instead, it starts to tell you what to do and what not to do and how to think about what you've just done. *Who does he think he is? I'll show him who's right! Why did I hit "send"? She's going to be so mad at me. I should have said . . . He's not listening to me; I worked so hard on this, and I'm losing his attention.* And so on, and so on.

You would be amazed at how common the Critic is among the senior leaders I work with. At first, it's not an easy thing for them to talk about, and I have to draw it out of them gently. Some feel ashamed to even acknowledge the Critic's existence. Others assume that *everybody* has a tough Critic in their heads and that, while it's burdensome and annoying, it's not particularly remarkable—so why talk about it? Many have tried without success to get rid of it and have given up, concluding that *this voice is me.* Conversely, others believe that it's the Critic that has made them successful. The Critic's voice is what gets them into overdrive, insists that they do more, push harder, rethink the plan, second-guess themselves, and so on, and so on. Many people in this last group fear that if my coaching works and I do something magical that chases the Critic away, they will *lose their edge.*

Let's not let me off the hook here. Looking back twenty years or so, back when I was trying *so hard* to turn myself into a successful strategy consultant, my Critic held center stage. When I did something at work that elicited a negative reaction from the team, my fear of being rejected was fully triggered: *Oh my God, what if I get pushed away from the team? Should I have said this? Should I have done this, or should I do it this way?* And all the while, there was this voice rumbling in my head, saying, *You need to send this email. Call this other person.* And years before, with my girlfriend: *Oh my God, I've screwed up; now I'm going to lose her!* And later with my wife, *Oh my God, I'm going to hear about it this time!* The Critic keeps right on talking: *If you don't do this, yeah, you will get fired, dumped, kicked out of the house.*

And then there's the voice of the Impostor. This one is well documented in the psychological literature, under the label "impostor syndrome." It's even made its way into the literature of management. The *Harvard Business Review*, for example, defines the impostor syndrome as a collection of feelings of inadequacy that persists despite evident success.[2] By all outward appearances, you're succeeding—maybe even big-time—but you're not internalizing that success, believing in yourself, or celebrating that success. You feel like a fake.

How does this happen? Think back to the belief system, described above. Many leaders of organizations come from very humble backgrounds—an origin story that's never very far from their minds. When they grow into positions of great power and responsibility, they hear that voice in their head saying, *Why me? All these people around me are better educated, have seen more of the world, know the cultural setting better than me,* and so on. *Maybe the fact of me sitting in this corner office is some kind of terrible mistake. Maybe they'll find me out!*

Even those clients who've enjoyed every privilege growing up may find themselves listening to the Impostor from time to time as well. They feel they haven't achieved enough through their own efforts to deserve it. This perception comes with a guilt triggered by the belief that their peers' journey to the top has been far more difficult—which inevitably translates into, *They are more deserving of the top position than I am.*

For both the Critic and the Impostor (and some others), these voices are *real*, and when we get overwhelmed, they can send us down to new lows—not the ideal mindset from which to lead! When people who are beset by one of these voices walk into the boardroom, a meeting with the executive committee, a session with clients, or a senior leadership huddle, they are seeing themselves as smaller than they really are, and less deserving—even when, in fact, they're perfectly capable of holding their own, and then some. Who am I talking about? I'm talking about the leaders of many $10-plus billion companies. They were plenty talented enough to win the job fair and square, and even so, they suspect in their hearts that a mistake has been made. Consequently, they will do far more work than anyone else—to an extent that, if not properly addressed, will almost certainly drive people crazy and ensure themselves a short tenure.

These voices, along with others that I could add to the list, are a key part of our psychological self-defense system. But this is a system that can become increasingly ineffective as you become more and more overwhelmed by life's pressures.

What happens when you feel your defenses starting to collapse and fear begins to enter into the picture? That's when human biology kicks in, leading to one of three mostly involuntary reactions: *freeze, flight,* or *fight.* Freeze doesn't work for long—our long-ago predators were generally able to spot us or sniff us out while we were frozen in place pretending to be tree trunks—so the real choice faced by most of us comes down to this: *flight* or *fight*?

## FIGHTING AND NOT FIGHTING

Most of the people whom I advise are *fighters* rather than people who flee from their fears. And yet, "fighters" often find ways to sidestep a fight. They step into a role that may work in the short term but is doomed to fail in the longer term.

For example, there's a group I call the Escapists. These are the people who generally procrastinate endlessly and thereby avoid having difficult conversations or making decisions they find stressful. You've certainly encountered otherwise competent leaders who simply refused to face the fact that Manager X had to be sent packing. Instead, you hear something like, "The company owes Mary so much; let's put our heads together and find her another role." Or if those hesitant leaders finally admit the inevitable—*Mary has to go*—they outsource the dirty work to someone else.

Maybe you don't believe that the leader of a giant corporation could get away with being an Escapist. Believe it. Here's a telltale clue: if leaders use their chief of staff to deal with awkward emotional business or family matters—the conversation with a difficult kid or distraught wife, for example—then they are deep into Escapism. There are a lot of Escapists out there. Despite their professional success, they step sideways whenever they have to deal with emotional conversations. They focus instead on the objective, factual challenges, like shaping corporate strategy and responding to operational challenges that aren't emotionally fraught.

Escapists who carry that role to an extreme have made an art of being physically present and quite functional—they *appear* to be listening very diligently—but in reality they become an Invisible Person. The Invisible Person tends to be someone who got into a leadership role simply out of sheer brilliance—no contest, the smartest person in the room, *always*. The Invisible Person is like a black hole: taking everything in, and shedding very little light on the subject at hand. This stance works in a lot of circumstances, but it fails in others. When the board chair demands an answer to a straightforward question, being invisible—even stepping sideways into *deeper* invisibility—is not likely to work. Reality keeps pounding on the door.

It's true: no matter how high you climb, there will almost certainly be someone whose job will be to protect the checks and balances, to hold the mirror up to you. And sooner or later, you'll be forced to confront those blind spots that you've been consciously—or even worse, unconsciously—trying not to learn about.

There are at least three more Fight archetypes that turn out to be more or less impossible stances to sustain: the Dutiful, the Perfectionist, and the Superhero.

The Dutiful is the person who copes with stress by working 24/7. This person is going to die in the saddle. It's the person who works Saturdays, Sundays, holidays, and so-called vacations. These people generally recognize no work-life boundaries—which of course means that their subordinates are also living a one-dimensional kind of life, working weekends and holidays. There are always rational-sounding excuses for this—*I need to get the strategy in place; I inherited a B-Team and can't do anything until I turn them around; it's not in our company culture for a leader to have a supporting system*; and so on—but all are excuses. There's trouble down below the waterline, but the Dutiful person may not even acknowledge that the waterline exists.

The Perfectionist is just what it sounds like: the person who demands perfection. It starts with *self*-perfection—everything I do is going to be absolutely flawless!—and ripples out from there, creating overwork in all directions. (That's when you start to hear things like, "I don't ask anything from them that I wouldn't ask of myself!") That leader is setting an impossibly high bar. And what happens when that bar gets cleared? You know all too well: the bar gets raised! *Now we have an even more impossible standard to meet!*

The Superhero is just like in the comic books, except that *our* Superheroes don't actually possess superpowers; they just wish they did and act like they would if only they had them. Faster than a speeding bullet, more powerful than a locomotive, able to leap tall buildings in a single bound: this is the stuff of fantasy, and yet it's the kind of standard to which Superheroes hold themselves. They think they have to do everything heroically, by themselves: *If I don't do it, it's not going to work out!* They're impatient with the mere mortals around them. They never ask for help. At an extreme, they're afraid of saying, "I don't know the answer to that question"—or worse, "I don't understand that question." Superheroes believe that asking for help demonstrates weakness, and real leaders *never* show weakness.

## GAINING FREEDOM OF CHOICE

When we are controlled by our emotions, we lose our ability to manage our energy. So instead, we tend to focus on managing our time. Well, guess what? It doesn't work. There is never enough time. We fail to reach our full potential. We start to make bad choices. In the worst case, we engage in self-hatred.

But self-hatred is absolutely the wrong note on which to end this chapter! Let me get to the same end point using more positive language.

Whenever we figure out what is holding us back, on a psychological level—whenever we achieve a conscious understanding of these deep things that are generally unconscious—our ability to love ourselves increases. When that happens, our confidence in ourselves grows, and as a result, we gain freedom of choice. We gain the ability to manage our energy, rather than our time. There is never enough time, but there is an unlimited amount of energy that you can tap into.

And when you do, the very things that once held you back now work for you—for your happiness and for your ability to create and achieve.

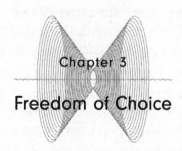

## Chapter 3

# Freedom of Choice

This chapter serves as a key point of transition on our journey. It's the gateway between the "what" section of this book and the "how." From this point on, we will be going down a path that isn't walked upon very often. Perhaps, as we dive deeper and deeper into connecting Eastern philosophies regarding energy management with the mindset of leaders in our Western culture, we will even be trailblazers.

Our focus starts with *freedom of choice*, which we amplify when we start to access *self*. Self is a person's essential being. It is the origin of our creative force. It is the place that we access when we are present and in complete peace and serenity. It's where our unlimited source of energy resides.

Simply stated, *we access self by expanding our self-awareness*. This is an essential aspect of learning how to be *more present*, which in turn helps you become a humane leader. Humane leaders are *self-confident* individuals. This may sound self-evident, but I think it's not. One complicating aspect is that *self-confident* is a concept that we're all used to hearing and saying. But take a minute to break "self-confidence" down into its component parts. It means, *having confidence in one's self*. And I'd add that *true* self-confidence is not a veneer. It's not the kind of temporary bump in your sense of well-being, your "self-esteem," that you get from, for example, putting on a new outfit, looking in the mirror, and deciding that you look sharp—ready to take on the world today! No; it's about a profound kind of awareness. It's about figuring out who your true "self" is and being comfortable with that person. And at a deeper emotional level, it's about being in a healthy relationship with yourself—and yes, *in love with yourself.* Why? Because from this place, there is no room for the Critic (described in chapter 2) to seize control. Your self-confidence is strong and grounded, and you are not only blessed with clarity of thought, you are also blessed with the ability to feel others' emotions and allow others to feel your emotions.

So, with that background in mind, let me share with you two brief stories about Dhanurjay "DJ" Patil, an off-the-charts smart mathematician and data scientist. He contributed significantly to the platforms that underlie eBay, PayPal, and LinkedIn. He also helped launch a successful start-up, RelateIQ, which was acquired by Salesforce, and was appointed by President Obama as the USA's first chief data scientist. (In fact, according to some accounts, DJ co-coined the phrase *data scientist.*) I've had the privilege of coaching DJ Patil for several years, and—full disclosure—I'm proud that he now considers me a friend.

So here's the first story. As you can imagine, DJ was (and still is) very hard for people to get to without an invitation. My firm understood that challenge all too well: we had tried many times to connect with him, all without success. My particular executive search niche focuses on connecting disruptive technologists with globally complex organizations, and one of our clients very much wanted me to help them find a way to make contact with DJ as a potential resource. So I decided to make a pitch to his heart. I wrote him an email with what I hoped was a provocative subject line—"Do you want to help Dona

Juana fund her crops?"—along with my contact information. Nothing more.

DJ replied within five minutes: "Who is Dona Juana and who are you?"

Nice! I quickly replied that Dona Juana is a Mexican farmer—true story—who lives ten miles away from the nearest bank, which makes it difficult for her to finance her crops. Meanwhile, I continued, there are seventy million mobile phones in Mexico, including Dona Juana's. Do you think you could find a way to help her? And by the way, I am Ricardo, and I have a client that's one of the biggest banks in the world, and they've asked me to get your help in thinking through this very tough challenge.

Again, DJ got back to me within five minutes: "Okay, I'm curious. Meet me at the yogurt shop on University Avenue in Palo Alto." That's how I got to know him. Since then, he's been advising my client with real impact, and I've been coaching him—which is how I learned this second story.

This story focuses on how DJ achieved his "overnight" success—which he's the first to say was far from overnight. He served as a research scientist and junior faculty member at the University of Maryland for almost a decade, where he applied new data-assimilation techniques to National Weather Service data to greatly improve forecasting. Then, in 2006, he and his family moved to Silicon Valley, where he landed a job at eBay as a research scientist focused on strategy, analytics, and product.

After only a short time into his work at eBay, somehow, a senior executive at PayPal—one of the eBay companies—got wind that there was some guy in the (figurative) basement who was rumored to be a really great problem-solver. PayPal was then struggling with several of its core technologies and needed help in a hurry. The executive (I'll call him Eric) set up a meeting with DJ and—after what DJ recalls was a very short conversation—made him the leader of a complex transformational project, thereby catapulting him up several ranks within the organizational structure.

In other words, both sides were taking a risk. It paid off. In less than a year, DJ came through with four major products that won awards and saved the company millions of dollars. One day in the wake of this success, DJ asked Eric why he had chosen to roll the dice on him in such a big way. The response he got was unexpected. "I knew about your reputation for solving big and complex problems," Eric replied, "and it was clear that you were smart enough. But I took that risk because of the way you made me feel during our conversation. You were humble, empathetic, vulnerable, and obviously a team player. It was all those human qualities, as well as your self-confidence, that made me feel that you would be the right choice. So, even though my head was telling me there was no way I should give such a big job to this relatively junior unknown, my heart was asking, *What are you waiting for?*"

Why did DJ enjoy outstanding career success, especially from that turning point onward, and become a humane leader? Where did his grounded self-confidence come from? How was he able to get his mind and emotions out of the way, access self, and amplify his creative superpower?

## THE POWER OF LEARNING HOW TO ACCESS SELF

Where do great leaders get the self-confidence that they need to take risks? Eric, that sage leader I described just above, delegated a difficult and important task to the relative newcomer DJ. Would Eric have done that if he wasn't self-confident? I'm sure he wouldn't have. And look at it from DJ's point of view. Would he have achieved all these positions of influence in different industries and settings if he wasn't self-confident?

There's no single template, of course. Some people who are promoted into leadership positions never find the self-confidence they need and quickly lose their authority. Others are brimming over with a self-confidence that is ego-based—in other words, arrogance—which doesn't hold up very well under fire and which can't survive a sustained streak of poor performance.

Again, where does this self-confidence come from? A lucky few—a very rare few—seem to have had access to it as far back as they can remember. But if you're like most of the world, you don't have this kind of easy access to self-confidence, and you need to develop it. As we'll see in later chapters, most leaders have learned to mask their insecurities. Yes, they make the tough calls forcefully. But inside? Many fear that they're going to let other people down and thereby let themselves down. You don't want to live with that kind of fear. And, as you'll discover in this book, you don't *need* to.

In the corner offices, you are required to take risks and impose vulnerability on yourself. Taking risks and being vulnerable? That requires courage. That, in turn, requires self-confidence. And where does self-confidence come from? It comes from *connecting to self*—full stop. Getting that kind of access comes through a self-discovery journey and the self-awareness that results from it. Learning how to access self is the critical first step on the path.

## HOW TO GET YOUR BODY, MIND, AND EMOTIONS OUT OF THE WAY OF ACCESSING SELF

For those readers who have never tried to access self, figuring out who your true self is may sound easy. After all, you've grown up with and know a lot about that person already, right?

Actually, it's a real challenge and a never-ending journey. Think back to the notion of the emotional pattern that I introduced in chapter 1. When we find ourselves in an untenable situation from an emotional standpoint, our balancing system kicks in to help move us from that bad situation to an emotionally safer one. We come up with emotional balancing (coping) strategies and use them again and again—until they become our subconscious and, as such, part of *who we believe we are*.

Sometimes we can use fairly simple mind exercises to get a glimpse of the power of accessing self to help ourselves break out of unconscious and unhelpful behaviors and embrace new, desired ones.

Let me share a real story that can help us warm up: I had a client—let's refer to her as Alice—who was terrified of public speaking. She was convinced that she would *always* feel anxious every time she had to step in front of a crowd to speak. Experiencing a severe case of "brain freeze" in that situation was just how she was naturally wired, she thought, and that was that.

Then Alice got a new job that required her to do a lot of public speaking.

What to do? Based on some stories that other friends had told me, I suggested that she hire a speech coach, which she somewhat reluctantly did.

I ran into her several months later and asked how the new job was going and whether she had gotten any more comfortable with getting up in front of a crowd. *Great* and *yes*, she replied enthusiastically. She then described how the speech coach had put her through a series of simple exercises aimed at helping her. One of the most impactful of them involved an exercise that combined mental awareness with physical activity. She was asked to divide the nearly empty auditorium in which she was practicing into three sections: left, middle, and right. The coach arranged to have one person sitting alone in each section, maybe twenty rows back from the stage. He told my client to stand up at the podium and deliver a short speech that her staffers had recently written for her. But instead of just racing through it with her head down, as was her habit, she should stop and focus on the "audience member" off to her left—in a sense, delivering the gift of being present only to that individual—and make a distinctive gesture with a hand and arm as she resumed speaking. The fingers and thumb on that hand were to be extended out straight and held together, said the coach, and my friend was to pretend she was chopping wood, her hand starting up near her ear and swinging down on the horizontal, pointing her fingertips at the target, focusing on that one individual. *Chop.* Then she'd read some more, pause, look at the audience member in the center section, and repeat the exercise. *Chop.* Same thing a page or two later, focused on the audience member off to her right. *Chop.* Then back to the left, center, and right, left, center, right, until she reached the end of the speech.

"And here's the strange thing," she told me. "The first time I did it, I felt totally foolish. Like a robot standing up there, repeating this contrived gesture in a stiff and mechanical way. But the next time we did the exercise, it all felt a little more natural. The coach then snuck some more people into the seats. No problem. I kept chopping wood, although this time, maybe not so mechanically. And eventually, I was speaking to a pretty big crowd like it was nothing."

The point of this story? Connecting body and mind increases your levels of presence, self-awareness, and self-confidence. It can help you break out of a self-limiting belief that may simply be wrong—as in the case of my client telling herself, and believing about herself, that she would always suffer when forced to speak publicly. But what my client discovered, down beneath all that superficial terror, was that she had a real need to *connect*—otherwise, she felt like a fake. Once she was able to connect with her audience in an authentic way, she enjoyed public speaking and became very good at it. By tapping into her true self, she gained self-confidence.

Let's dig deeper. Let's look at how we can tap into our *minds*, *emotions*, and *bodies* to understand ourselves better and, by gaining access to our true selves, to lead more effectively and humanely.

## CENTERING YOUR MIND

Alice wasn't who she thought she was.

Through a focused and determined effort, she was able to silence her thoughts and thereby tap into an unexpected reserve of joy within herself. For her, this was a completely unexpected turn of events. By distracting and silencing her thoughts with motion, she got a clearer understanding of herself—and by tapping into that true self, she boosted her level of self-confidence and became a better public speaker. From that point forward, as long as she was able to connect with her audience, she actually enjoyed getting up and talking to a crowd.

To my mind, this was a compelling case of what I'll call "centering the mind." What does that mean? If you're of my generation or older, I'll invite you to remember what tuning a car radio used to involve or finding a radio station by adjusting the dial on the tuner on your home stereo. To the left or right of that station you were looking for, you'd hear fuzz, static, and maybe snippets of other stations floating in and out. Gradually, twisting the knob, *you centered* on the right wavelength. Centering the mind is just like this, but it turns the goal exactly the opposite. You're not seeking a certain noise but, instead, the *absence* of noise.

Easier said than done, but still doable. Alice brought her considerable intellect to bear on the challenge of understanding herself. She centered her mind. She examined where she was *in the present*, worked with a speech coach to arrive at a new way of doing things, and changed her context in ways that brought her into closer alignment with who she really was.

My contention here is that this kind of growth isn't limited to specific challenges—like the fear of public speaking—but *can be pursued more generally*, to create conscious awareness of your true self.

This involves a more holistic and systematic approach. Remember those chattering voices I described in the last chapter? One could say that those voices are your head spinning out of control. Part of the challenge of learning from your mind is figuring out how to silence these voices. It's paradoxical: in order to learn from your mind, you have to silence it. You need to be in the present.

The best way to do this is by distracting the mind—for example, through some form of breathing or with a focused way of moving like Alice did. Give conscious breathing a try. First, close your eyes. Then intentionally try to silence your mind by consciously breathing in through your nose and out through your mouth. Do this for one minute. As soon as thoughts come back into your mind, go back to conscious breathing. Try doing it daily for a week or so. Once you've nailed it, go to three minutes. Again, if thoughts pop up, go back to conscious breathing—but now add one more touch: place one hand on your heart and keep it there.

Be aware if this makes distracting your mind easier or more difficult. In my case, it makes it easier, because I find it relaxing to feel my own heartbeat.

To sum up: you center *your mind through silence*, and this practice will help you get there.

## CENTERING YOUR EMOTIONS

The next question we need to confront is what do you *do* with these lessons that you learn from centering your mind? It's not enough to gain access into your true self through the insights of the mind; you also have to *accept* those insights. This involves centering your *emotions*.

One of my mentors is a brilliant therapist named Richard "Dick" C. Schwartz. Dick Schwartz is the author of *Internal Family Systems Therapy*, and he's the one who taught me about the importance of centering your emotions to quiet down those voices that live inside us all. He points out that many traditional psychotherapeutic frameworks advocate getting rid of the Critic (my word). He argues, somewhat counterintuitively, that the Protector (his word) is a *good* thing. It arises out of pure love—the mechanism whereby young children with energy and imagination defend themselves in the most stressful of situations. "So let's not get rid of the Critic," Dick argues, in my paraphrase of this observation. "It has served you well. Let's honor it, thank it, and if it wants to stick around, let's give it a new job."

Here, let's apply Dick's insight more broadly. Through our upbringings, we create emotional balancing strategies that live within our bodies. Psychotherapists tend to call them "defense mechanisms." In traditional psychotherapy, the goal is to rid ourselves of these defense mechanisms because they're in the way of letting you truly be in control of your emotions—and therefore are preventing you from being truly free.

Dick Schwartz energetically disagrees with that approach. Instead, he argues that these defense mechanisms are there to take care of you. Rather than getting rid of them, you need to get into a new kind of relationship with them so they won't get in the way of your ability to love yourself or your ability to gain love from others.

Based on this insight, Dick Schwartz—being the family therapist that he is—created the Internal Family Systems (IFS) framework. This framework is intended to help you connect with your Protector(s), or defense mechanisms—in other words, to help you have productive conversations with your voices. It leads you through a series of immersive sessions to center your emotions through acceptance and, by doing so, gain greater access to self. A humane leader leads from self.

An IFS practitioner is therefore less like a traditional therapist and more like an emotional-unconscious tour guide and translator, helping you connect to defense mechanisms and helping you to understand them, heal them, and *accept* them. I always liked the mental image of checking all your emotional bags curbside at the airport, allowing you to board your plane unencumbered to embark on a journey of self-discovery. Having your emotional "hands" free makes acceptance so much easier!

Emotional acceptance is very difficult to achieve on your own. Yes, you can give it a try, but keep in mind that when you're no longer able to continue answering the question *Why do I behave this way?* that's a clue that you've hit a wall and would probably benefit from some additional support. If you decide to seek that support, there are many practices and approaches out there to help you. The most sophisticated and effective practices I have come across and use with my clients are Internal Family Systems—described above, and searchable online—and Family Constellations, which I'll describe in chapter 7.

To sum up: you center your emotions through acceptance.

## CENTERING YOUR BODY

The third dimension that provides a critical point of access into your true self is your body. Centering your body is about embodying wisdom—literally.

This notion sometimes surprises my clients: "My body is a repository and source of wisdom?" they ask. Yes, I tell them— very much so, even though our Western culture doesn't give you many clues in this direction.

In a hilarious and provocative TED talk, British deep thinker and author Sir Ken Robinson talks about how university professors are viewed by the educational system as the absolute pinnacle of success—and also about how *odd* they are. "They live in their *heads*," he says:

> They live *up there*, and slightly to one side. They're disembodied, in a kind of literal way. They look upon their body as a form of transport for their heads. It's a way of getting their heads to meetings.
>
> If you want real evidence of out-of-body experiences, by the way, get yourself along to a residential conference of senior academics and pop into the discotheque on the final night. And there you will see it. Grown men and women writhing uncontrollably, off the beat. Waiting until it ends, so they can go home and write a paper about it.[1]

I first heard this Ken Robinson quote paraphrased by a dynamic and complicated sage named Scott Coady.[2] I was then working with Scott on a program offered through my firm. I was impressed with Scott's wisdom and depth—which I later came to think of as his embodied presence—and eventually asked him if he'd be willing to coach me. He pretty much said no to that, saying that he wasn't really a coach. But if I were interested, he continued, he would walk me through the kinds of things that might be holding me back and preventing me from getting access to my wisest self—"the spark within," as I think he phrased it. *That* sounded even more promising, and I immediately accepted.

What I learned directly from Scott Coady, and indirectly through programs offered by his Institute for Embodied Wisdom, had to do with (as he calls it) *getting the body into the learning*. Scott starts making his case by stating, simply, that we humans are a certain kind of mammal—specifically, a social/hierarchical mammal, like dogs, horses, elephants, and dolphins—and that we embody ("build into our bodies") all kinds of wisdom that helps make us effective in this kind of society. We need to understand that process of embodiment, Scott says. Once we do, we can *change* our embodiment:

> My work has been all about helping people shift the embodiment that they are to be more aligned with the vision or commitment they have for the future. When those two things are lined up, it's pretty powerful.

For example? Well, to cite a simple example, how about riding a bike? You can't ride a bike until you try it and master it—and once you do, you never forget that fairly elementary nugget of embodied wisdom. Another example: Scott sometimes invites his friendly skeptics to stand, or sit, with their arms at their sides and then he asks them to cross their arms. They do. (Try it yourself, in real time.) Then he asks them to *cross their arms the other way*. Not so easy—because by doing so, they are running against their muscle memory, which is their embodied wisdom.

Again, that's an elementary nugget, and not particularly robust. But by invoking it, Scott makes the point that there's a whole world of subtle, nuanced, and powerful kinds of wisdom that add up to embodied intelligence.

There's another word for it: *intuition*. People who can tap into the intelligence of their bodies have "good instincts." They "trust their guts." And trust is the coin of the realm when it comes to leadership, says Scott: "You have to be able to manufacture trust authentically if you're going to lead." And this is the beautiful thing about embodied wisdom, he continues: "It can help us develop authentic self-confidence that's grounded and rooted in the body."

To look at this from another angle, think about the opposite circumstance: a *lack* of self-confidence that's grounded in the body. We are told not to show fear to angry dogs or bears because that will make them more likely to attack. This is a bit of an exaggeration, but it's been proven that, at the very least, dogs use their noses and eyes to pick up on your "fear cues" and become more fearful themselves. Isn't it likely that we humans, even despite the dominance and swagger of our big brains, possess similar somatic capabilities?[3]

Can you recall a time when you walked into a room and felt that you could "cut the tension with a knife"? That was your body stepping forward to help you out. Can you remember a deal you walked away from because it "just didn't feel right"? Again, probably a good instinct. Can you bring to mind misleading leaders who—you sensed—weren't up to the task? The truth is, they weren't *comfortable in their skin*, as the old saying goes, and you picked up on it.

How do we get access to our wisest selves? When it comes to the body, the answer has many parts. The practice that I am about to describe is quite similar to the one I shared above, which was aimed at centering your mind. The difference lies in the *intention*. In that previous case, the intention was to *silence the mind*, while here, the intention is *connecting with your body*. With practice, you will do both at the same time. To get started, breathe, and watch yourself breathe. As you breathe, relax your body. Get off autopilot. Imagine an emotion—let's say anger—and repeat the phrase "I experience anger when . . . ," completing the sentence with a new ending each time. Keep doing this until you actually feel angry. When you get there, place a finger on the part of your body where you feel the anger and stay with it. (Don't stop the focused breathing; this is key.) Where your finger has landed is the place where anger lives in your body.

Now repeat the same process with another emotion in mind—such as grief, for example. Breathe. Repeat and finish the phrase "I experience grief when . . . ," and put your finger on the place where the grief starts to manifest itself. I suspect that you'll find that grief and anger live in different parts of your body. That's true for most of us, even though those locations are not the same for all of us. In my case, my anger resides in my jaw, while my grief resides in my gut.

Where do your emotions live in your body? Figuring that out is a terrific way to center your body and, ultimately, to connect to your embodied wisdom.

## A COMPLEX AND NONLINEAR PROCESS

I should offer a word of caution here. Words on a page are necessarily linear: one comes after another. But centering mind, body, and emotions to access self is not a linear practice. To keep it simple, you'll probably start by choosing the centering of one and stay there for a while—I mean, a few weeks or more—until you feel that you've got the hang of it.

I personally find it easier to start by centering the body (breathing) and then moving on to centering the mind (silence, often combined with breathing to distract the thoughts); and then moving on to emotional acceptance.

Keep in mind that getting access to self is quite complex. Mind, emotions, and body tend to connect themselves anyway, in ways that aren't always helpful. (Emotions can trigger counterproductive actions, for example.) So neither mind, emotions, nor body are all that helpful when they are tapped in isolation—but when they are effectively combined, they're *extremely* helpful.

Figure 1 was created by Scott Coady, who has kindly given me permission to reproduce it here. Note how the three circles intersect, and—at the center—create a space called "self." At the risk of repeating myself: when you center your mind through silence, and your emotions through acceptance, and

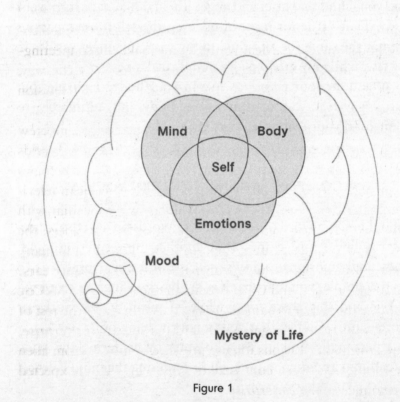

Figure 1

your body through breathing, you *get access to self*. And as I shared at the beginning of this chapter, self is a reservoir of unlimited energy, tying you into a reservoir of boundless wisdom and unconditional love. When we tap into that reservoir, we can connect completely with life. When we lead from self, we are being present; we are being humane leaders.

## CONNECTING TO SELF:
## A LESSON FROM THE STARSHIP *ENTERPRISE*

Self: Don't worry if you don't quite get it. It's not an easy concept.

Over the next few chapters, we're going to be building up toward the understanding of self, while we focus on mastering your energy, step-by-step, in ways that you'll find comprehensible and compelling. Meanwhile, let me make my connecting-to-self point by leveraging pop culture—which, by the way, I love. In this case, I draw on the original *Star Trek* television series.

That show presented the adventures of a heterogeneous crew on a five-year space mission to explore strange new worlds and seek out new life-forms and civilizations. My apologies in advance to readers who weren't watching American television in the 1960s and 1970s and therefore aren't familiar with *Star Trek*. A quick recap for the benefit of those readers: the three main characters were Captain James T. Kirk (a human), Science Officer Spock (a Vulcan with distinctive pointy ears, signaling "alien"), and Chief Medical Officer Leonard McCoy (another human, nicknamed "Bones"). As they and the rest of the crew explored the galaxy aboard the starship *Enterprise*, they came under various intense pressures—mostly from alien life-forms that were confused or upset by the unexpected appearance of the *Enterprise*.

What was interesting, at least to me, was how these three individuals responded to those intense pressures. In a gratifying way, they embody the archetypes introduced above. For example, Spock was The Mind: totally logical, rational, composed, linear, seemingly bloodless. He interacted extremely well, almost intimately, with the ship's computer. Cool under fire, he was excellent at hypothesizing what was actually going on in almost any desperate moment and presenting a logical way for the *Enterprise* to wriggle its way out of the mess it was in.

But somehow, we viewers knew he shouldn't be trusted to take "the conn": *Star Trek* jargon for taking control of the ship. Yes, he was an invaluable resource and forceful presence on the bridge of the ship. But he was also astoundingly one-dimensional—and therefore, we knew, not the leader the ship would need in a crisis.

Bones was The Emotions. He wore his heart on his sleeve. Argumentative and irascible, he was inclined to blurt out what was on his mind—which was usually driven by feelings rather than logic. His bedside manner was prickly rather than loving, but we understood that he cared deeply about his patients down in the sick bay. Whenever he got the chance, he carped at Spock for being so *unfeeling*. (Spock couldn't have cared less.) He disapproved of risk-taking and acts of boldness because they put people he cared for—even Spock—in danger. Outside of the sick bay, Bones was not a leader. He never took the conn, or came close to it.

Finally, Captain Kirk was primarily The Body. Yes, he was a focused thinker and a canny strategist, sometimes surprising even Spock with the power of his supposedly inferior human intellect. But at the same time, he was highly intuitive and even visceral—always getting into shoot-outs, fistfights, and torrid love affairs. Although he was a little too quick to throw a punch, he certainly benefited from the kind of embodied wisdom that Scott Coady advocates.

But let me go a step further out onto the thin ice. To a limited extent, Kirk was able to tap into Mind, Emotion, and Body and get them out of the way—in other words, he was in touch with his *self*. Even with his limitations, he exuded competence and self-confidence. He led bravely, decisively, and humanely. His polyglot crew followed him into seriously bad situations, again and again, without hesitation.

Subsequent starship commanders in the *Star Trek* franchise dialed back Kirk's beefy pugnaciousness—The Body—and therefore presented a more balanced persona to the universe. But what was interesting about that unfolding drama, series by series, was the evolution of what I'd call the *mood* of the story.

Look back at figure 1. Around the edges of that diagram is a fuzzy sort of cloud labeled "mood." Kirk understood that he was something special and played an important role in writing his own leadership story—creating the *mood* around his leadership. And yet he also understood that there were some things that he was never going to be able to control—or even understand. But rather than struggle pointlessly against the unknowable, he simply surrendered to his limitations and moved on. Paradoxically, by acknowledging the limits on his power, Kirk actually *enhanced* his power.

Kirk's successors on the bridge of the *Enterprise* in later series also understood this paradox. They acknowledged that there was more than one author involved in writing their story and that the mystery of life hinged on surrendering to the limits of one's own power, influence, and control. The moods they created around their leadership tenures were different, but those moods were subordinate to bigger forces at work in the universe.

## WHAT'S NEXT?

To sum up: it's about *centering* and *connecting*, into self. Again, we center our minds through silence. We center our emotions through acceptance. We center our bodies through breathing. And through hard work within each of these dimensions, we connect them, *and* get them out of the way—and thereby gain access to self. Getting there gives us immense freedom of choice. It lets us contribute to the (mood) writing of our story, rather than letting others write it for us, and enhances our ability to lead in a humane way.

I should say again that this is hard work, and it's not always fun work. It's something you build up to gradually, and carefully. In my home country of Mexico, cantinas (equivalent of a pub or a bar) sometimes rent their customers what's called a *maquina de toques* (Spanish for "electric shock machine"). It's basically a small battery with two metal handles attached to it, and it administers an electric shock to patrons who grab those handles. If you come across a *maquina de toques* and decide to try it, I recommend that you *not* start at a high voltage level, because you'll wind up on your posterior. But at the same time, it's something that you can build up to. I imagine that the bucking-bronco machines in bars in the USA were created with the same idea in mind: *build up to it*.

Is all that hard and sometimes painful work worth it? Yes. Gaining access to our true selves, in turn, builds our self-confidence, and with that comes greater freedom of choice. As you'll see, much of the language that we'll use on the path to humane leadership is about gaining access to, and managing, energy.

# Part II

# Mastering the Seven Levels

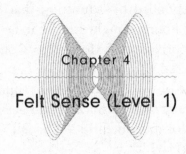

## Chapter 4

# Felt Sense (Level 1)

Rising from his desk in his corner office overlooking the Swiss Alps, Emile Dorantz—the CEO of a global Fortune 100 company—greeted me in his usual way: with a warm embrace, followed by thoughtful questions about my work and family.[1]

Emile had been in the CEO role for more than a year at that point. A few months back, he decided that he wanted to consult with me about what he perceived to be his time-management challenges. Based on several of our ensuing conversations, I began to see a bigger challenge: Emile had significant problems setting boundaries, and—as the CEO of a globally complex organization—he had to fix this larger problem *quickly* or risk getting burned out.

Emile readily agreed with my broader definition of his challenge. He agreed that his role as a company-wide resource had become all consuming. Now, he said, he wanted to discover a way to carve out what he called "pockets of freedom" to take care of himself, while still delivering the level of performance expected by the company's investors.

I encouraged him to tell me more. "What would you like to do," I asked him, "if you succeed at carving out these pockets of freedom? What would be different?"

Emile first responded by admitting that he was sleeping only four to five hours a night and that he was feeling the effects of sleep deprivation. "More sleep would be good," he said. He remembered, too, that before he became CEO, he had a morning routine of working out before going to the office—but it had been many months since he had been able to do that.

I asked Emile for more details: "What's your typical work-day routine, currently?"

Given his admission about being sleep deprived, I wasn't surprised when he started his recitation of his daily routine with his late-evening activity: clearing his email inbox and messages, which sometimes took several hours. Then he'd get to bed sometime before midnight, toss and turn for a while, and then (hopefully) log a few hours of sleep. Then he'd wake up around 5:00 a.m., check his email and messages while having a quick breakfast, and head straight to the office, usually arriving there before seven. Mornings and afternoons were typically a blur of meetings and conference calls, interrupted by a quick lunch at the coffee table in his office, although more often than not he was joined by colleagues for a spontaneous brown-bag working lunch—an informal tradition that he had encouraged. By midafternoon, he confessed, he generally felt pretty tired, and he suspected that he wasn't thinking as clearly as he had even several hours earlier.

"So when do you get to rest and renew?" I asked.

"Honestly, I guess I don't," he said. "Sometimes on the weekend, maybe."

Not a good routine, to put it mildly! If Emile continued down this particular track, with work dominating his life and threatening his health, he was going to get derailed.

Our conversations continued. Learning from Emile about what gave him energy and what stole his energy away turned out to be a relatively straightforward process of discovery. Not only was he an open book; he was also quite self-aware and relatively connected to his energy flows. Again, that was the easy part. What *wasn't* so easy was getting down to the root cause of what was holding him back and preventing him from setting the kinds of boundaries that would allow him to create these "pockets of freedom" he was envisioning.

"When you feel the frustration of not being able to create these pockets of freedom," I asked him, "where in your body do you feel it?"

This time he was stumped. He thought and thought and finally shared that he actually didn't remember the last time he felt emotions in his body. Yes, he recalled with a smile, he certainly felt butterflies back when he was dating his future wife—but that was a long, long time ago! He volunteered that he wasn't afraid of the prospect of exploring within himself. But, as he frankly admitted, he just couldn't connect with this question of where in his body he felt frustration: "Frankly, Ricardo, I've always assumed that my emotions lived in my *mind*. Maybe I just have a blind spot when it comes to this feeling-energy-in-my-body stuff."

I replied, politely but firmly, that if he really wanted to create these pockets of freedom, it would be essential for him to reconnect to his body. Why? Because the answer to his question was to be found in his body, not in his mind. "You've been knocking on the wrong door," I said.

We agreed to put that particular discussion on hold until our next meeting, a couple of weeks out. But before I left, I gave Emile homework. He agreed to get at least seven hours of sleep per night, *no matter what*. He further agreed that when he woke up in the morning, he would do his exercise routine before tackling his virtual inboxes. I also asked him to start getting more in touch with his body, in ways that he could relate to. For example, I encouraged him to feel the physical pleasure that's inherent in the process of getting to sleep and that is a component of a good workout. I then raised the antenna a bit with the following request: Every time you feel the need to work on your inbox in a way that conflicts with your mandatory seven-hour sleep window, or every time you feel compelled to open that inbox at dawn before your workout, ask yourself the following question:

Where in my body do I feel the need to do this?

And once you're able to pinpoint that place in your body—which you will be able to do, by the way!—ask yourself this question:

*Why* do I need to do this?

By this point in the conversation, he was again looking at me a little sideways. I simply asked him to trust me and to be prepared to report back his findings in our next session.

Emile is by nature an open and curious person, drawn to new ideas, and so I wasn't at all surprised to learn a couple of weeks later that he had taken his homework very seriously. From the first moment I saw him, he looked *different*. His face seemed to be a healthier color. It felt different to be in the room with him. He was *energized*, almost brimming over with confidence and optimism. He immediately jumped up and came across the office to shake my hand. "Ricardo," he began, omitting our normal opening chitchat, "so glad to see you!"

As we took our seats at the coffee table, he continued. "I must admit that when we concluded our last session, I was feeling quite frustrated with you. And frankly, quite skeptical—I mean, how can an answer be in my body? But wow! I'm happy to report, first, that I feel rested and better able to solve more problems just as a result of feeling less tired. But in answer to the question I know you're going to ask me—yes! To my surprise, whenever I was tempted to go back to my inbox late at night or in the early morning and asked myself your first question, I was able to feel a hole in my stomach. I'm not sure if it was frustration or anxiety or whatever, but it was *there*. And as soon as I focused on my abdomen and asked myself, *Why do I need to do this?* I realized that I have a big fear of *letting people down*.

"Well, after that, I found it relatively easy to focus on that spot, and on that realization, and let go of the need to always be tending to my inbox. For sure, I wasn't perfect. But at least I was able to place some boundaries and begin protecting my time better. So what's next? Can I unlock more physical energy through my body? What do we *do* with this information?"

And that was in the first two minutes of our session! I laughed and held up both hands in a "stop the traffic" motion. "Whoa, whoa, Emile! First, let's honor this moment. You've just hit upon an important discovery—the root cause of what most likely has been keeping you from creating those pockets of freedom you've been talking about. You've found a way to reclaim your body's energy and get it flowing again. That's a big deal, and it's something we need to take the time to celebrate!"

Of course Emile wanted to plunge right into the next phase of his journey. That impatience to *get on with it* is part of what has made him so successful professionally. But it's also one of the reasons why his body was numb in the first place. So we deliberately slowed down, took some time to celebrate the "arrival" of Emile's body and its abundant energy, and agreed to pick up his truly momentous discovery—his fear of letting people down—in our upcoming sessions.

I'll return to Emile's story, and the next round of discoveries he made on his journey, in the next chapter.

## THE BODY AND SENSATIONS

*Cogito, ergo sum:* I think, therefore I am.

Seventeenth-century philosopher René Descartes coined this phrase as part of a bigger exploration of how we humans can attain knowledge that is *certain* and logically unassailable. For better or worse, over the past few centuries we humans have mostly missed his point. Today, we understand Descartes's assertion to mean that our existence is rooted in our minds, that our bodies are not part of our "am-ness," and that our two parts—mind and body—are separate and unequal.

As Emile's case illustrates, we need to regain access to the energy inherent in our bodies. To get there, we need to redeem and elevate our physical beings. With all due apologies to Descartes: *I am, therefore I think.*

"Body" comes from the old English *bodig*, or *botah*, meaning "vessel." The bodig was the container within which the alchemist tried to turn lead into gold. This is both a bad and a good metaphor. On the one hand, our bodies aren't just empty vessels awaiting orders from that pushy globe on top of our shoulders. On the other hand, I like the image of our bodies as transformational vessels—that is, as vehicles of creativity, with the capacity to generate things beyond the known and, in fact, beyond our wildest imaginations. How can this be? Imagine that you are a plant. Your roots stabilize you, take in your food, and store your reserves. Now go back to normal— to being a human in a body. Your body is where you develop the capacity for generative nourishment. You need a healthy body to nourish your physical, mental, emotional, and spiritual energy flow.

The first level of the human energy field (HEF) is associated with the functioning of our physical body and especially our physical sensations.[2] Our need at this level is to maintain a healthy body and enjoy all the wonderful sensations in the body that come with that state of health.

This is the realm of the senses. It's super important. Our senses—smell, sight, touch, taste, hearing—are what connect us to the world. We are at our best when we are well connected to the world. This, in turn, happens when our senses are at their best—which they can only be if we are physically healthy.

The prescriptions that grow out of this succession of seemingly simple observations may seem obvious: *Sleep well. Eat well. Breathe well. Take care of yourself.* But is this really so obvious? Was it obvious to Emile, at first?

What do we humans get a physical charge out of? (When you think about it, that's an interesting turn of phrase, right?) Well, certainly we get a charge out of good food, comfortable and beautiful surroundings, physical contact with our significant others, a deep and restful sleep, a romp with the dog, that loving hug from a child or grandchild, the endorphins that are released by vigorous physical exercise, and so much more.

"Climb the mountains and get their good tidings," wrote naturalist John Muir. "Nature's peace will flow into you as sunshine flows into trees. The winds will blow their own freshness into you, and the storms their energy, while cares will drop away from you like the leaves of Autumn."[3]

*Cares dropping away*: sounds perfect.

## BRINGING THE POWER
## OF INTENTIONALITY IS ESSENTIAL

When used right, intentionality is more than just a wish; it's a magic wand.

In 1978, Shakti Gawain published a compact, well-written book titled *Creative Visualization*.[4] I admit that I approached it with modest expectations, in part because I was still in the midst of my own journey of discovery, but I started reading, and pretty soon I was won over.

Gawain calls upon three elements that together can help make intentions into realities. She's not dogmatic about how that should happen, other than to say that you have to bring three elements to bear:

1. **Desire**. Do I truly, in my heart, desire this goal to be realized?
2. **Belief**. Do I believe that it's possible for me to make this happen?
3. **Acceptance**. Am I completely willing to take its consequences?

In other words, your intentionality takes the form of a true desire, is based on the belief that you can realize that desire, and reflects your full acceptance of what may come. Once that intentionality becomes clear, you have "waved the magic wand," in effect.

Yes, *what* you do is important—but *why* you do it is equally important. Engaging in *meditation with intention* as a daily practice is a very powerful way to enhance your ability to amplify your felt sense and manage your energy at Level 1. Too many people attempt to meditate without knowing how to go about it. Take me, for example: I started trying to learn how to meditate without a clear objective, which meant that I was soon tempted to move on and try something else. A meditation with intention, by contrast, accelerates and amplifies our ability to shift our energy and, accordingly, our personality patterns. When this happens, energy is liberated—and our ability to manage it and create with it is greatly enhanced.

This is very much the case on Level 1, even though the disciplines that you need to follow on this level are relatively simple. On Level 1, your intention is to enhance your ability to feel pleasure by taking care of yourself. You're not just eating out of habit or because you're bored or because something fresh out of the oven smells pretty good. You're eating with the *intention* of enjoying your meal.

Similarly with sleeping: it's not intentional enough to sleep because you want to be rested or because it's hot outside or because you've found a welcoming place to lie down. If your intention for being rested is to be at your best to feel more pleasure, to feel and enjoy life, yes—take that nap! But again: do so as part of your bigger picture of intention.

You'd be amazed at how many of my clients don't get this when we start. I ask them, as I asked Emile, "How many hours of sleep do you get a night, on average?" A common answer is five to six hours. Then I ask if that's because they've chosen five hours as the right amount of sleep to get if they want to be energized and feel more connected to the world the following day. "Of course not," they say, in so many words. "But the committee meetings at the end of the day tend to run long, and I usually have some paperwork to do after dinner, and I often have to get in early for such-and-such," and so on.

Sorry: *you can't be purposeful about working if you're not purposeful about sleeping.* If you want to carry out your important tasks well, a smaller number of minutes of you at your sharpest is *far better* than more minutes of you sleep-deprived and fuzzy.

This is a subtle difference, which probably doesn't conflict with anything you are currently doing to sleep well or stay fit. With practice, you will not only amplify your ability to connect through your senses, you also will be less tired, which is a key benefit when you learn how to be in your body and to "center" in your physical dimension.

Maybe to your ears "taking care of our physical energy with the intention of feeling pleasure in everything we do with our senses" sounds like a distinction without a difference. After all, aren't you taking the same nap, eating the same stuff, and burning the same calories even without a larger intention in mind? In one sense, the answer is *yes*. Your Fitbit can't tell the difference between a random calorie burned and an intentional calorie burned. But on a deeper level, the answer is *no*. Transforming your practice from "just doing something" to doing something purposeful—action with intention—is *an essential shift in outlook*. It's a shift toward changing and managing the energy of what you are doing. When you succeed at realizing your intention, you will access greater levels of physical strength and health, which is a solid foundation on which to build greater levels of self-confidence, improved clarity of thought, and enhanced freedom of choice and, eventually, to tap into deep levels of creative power and energy.

## BEING PRESENT IN THE MOMENT

Many people conduct their professional lives in a way that's designed to sidestep Level 1. They avoid connecting with their physical selves. They are mounting a vain effort to avoid feeling pleasure—especially during work hours—and maybe to avoid feeling anything at all. "That's why I have a personal life, right"? one of them asked me, a little defensively.

Let's turn this on its head. Why in the world would we human beings believe that staying numb for many hours of the day is fine? It makes no sense. And yet, many senior business leaders believe it. They tell me that, at work, physical sensations (especially pleasurable ones) have to be left behind, because you need to "stay sharp." This is very bad wiring—a short circuit if you will. These hardworking leaders are so afraid of being "distracted" that they're overloading their wiring, which of course increases their chances of failing.

Some of my clients try to go a level deeper by embracing some sort of discipline at Level 1 but at the same time fending off any notion of intentionality. For example: "Working out helps me take my mind off work." Well, okay; but exercise without an intention is often a way of numbing yourself—and that's almost *exactly backward*. You need your energy, and your mind, to be *on* at home and at work. And for that to happen, you need to be able to tap into the power of being present in your body.

Why is being present in your body so important? Again, it is a prerequisite for gaining access to the unlimited source of energy within your human energy field. By being in your body, you can learn how to *feel* your body. Think back to Emile's example. Feeling sensations in your body enables you to start having a felt sense of your emotions, which is an essential ingredient to help you find where blocked energy flow is held in your body; without proper energy flow in your body, you can't access self. In the extreme case, you will ultimately fall sick or inhibit your ability to perform and your ability to create. We will learn in subsequent chapters how to shift the energy of these energy blockers.

Another name for these energy blockers is trauma. What makes trauma, trauma? The term comes from the Greek word for *wound*. Trauma is the body's response to a life-threatening event; it is a freeze in the flow of the body's natural responses and therefore a disruption in the flow of our body energy. The root cause of trauma is an experience that disrupts and interferes with our inherent need for safety, belonging, and dignity. It can result either from a single incident or from circumstances that persist over time. As I explained in chapter 2, your fear system is created in response to this incident or these circumstances as a protective mechanism, to avoid experiencing the pain again.

Energy blockers take root in our bodies and wait for an opportune moment to arise and demand a remedy. In other words, when something in our current circumstances reminds us of a past threatening experience (whether it was perceived or real), we are likely to get triggered. And since these experiences live in our body, we are very likely to react in the present in the same ways that we did in the past. Smells, textures, even a tone of voice: all can trigger a stress response that makes it very difficult for us to stay centered, to stay in the present. We may not even be *aware* of being triggered and therefore may have no clear understanding of why we have the sudden impulse to fight, flee, or freeze.

But we need to gain this awareness if we are to move forward on our journey. We need to first become aware of these energy blockers and triggers and be able to take a deep breath to get back in our bodies—and back to center. And then we need to tap into them to advance the healing process.

This isn't easy, and it's made more difficult by contemporary medical practice. Especially in Western cultures, trauma is often pathologized as a mental disorder. But mental disorder is a misnomer because everything emerges from and expresses itself in the body. Yes, there are mental symptoms, but they don't exist independent of the body's experience. Meanwhile, by focusing on mental disorder, we lose sight of the fact that these energy blockers present us with an open invitation into who we are meant to be. In other words, painful as they may be, they are indispensable tools. They provide us with a direct through line to gaining access to self and thereby access to our unlimited source of energy. Yes, these energy blockers are wounds, which left unattended can cause further harm. But when they are looked into, and looked after, we can move these parts of the body from a state of contraction toward a state of openness—to a state of well-being.

The path to healing our body is innate. We are all born with the capacity to transform ourselves, but when we lose connection with our embodied self, we reject the hidden gifts of these energy blockers. The answer lies in accepting that we have been harmed and that change is going to be hard, even scary and painful—but that this change is well worth it.

Let's go back to those obvious prescriptions, mentioned at the outset of the chapter. You need to *eat well.* And by that I mean, eat in a way that meets your needs and advances your intentions. It doesn't matter which diet you follow, as long as it's reasonably balanced; what matters is that you eat *with the intention to feel good and—as a result—to feel more pleasure.* That means focusing not only on what you eat but *how* you eat. It means being present in the moment as you eat. It does *not* mean microwaving something more or less at random and wolfing it down so that you can check the "lunch: 12:00 to 12:15" box on your daily agenda, all the while looking back with regrets at the last miscue of the morning or looking toward to the afternoon's impending calamity. Honestly, in most cases, if calamity is really around the corner, it can wait, right? This is your time for taking care of yourself.

Breathing is a super-important element of experiencing pleasure intentionally. Breathing is the best way to "center" the body, as described in previous chapters. Even though in Western culture we tend to talk almost constantly about eating, breathing is by far our biggest habit of consumption. We actually take in about fifteen pounds of air for every one pound of food we consume.

Even as I'm writing this, I'm trying to be mindful of how I am breathing. For me, this discipline begins early in the day, around dawn, with a ten-minute breathing exercise that helps me focus on being in the present. I highly recommend the Wim Hof method, but there are many others.[5] In the Japanese culture, breathing is a discipline that connects you to your life force, which they call Hara, based on breathing from your lower abdomen.[6] According to devotees of Hara, it takes a lifetime to master it—but when you do, you can unlock immense energy.

You can and should find your own routines, and I encourage you to do so. The exploration is half the fun and much of the discipline.

Back to where we started: if you practice setting your intention to feel pleasure in everything physical you do, you will soon experience greater levels of physical energy. It's that simple, and that profound. It's not easy, but with practice and patience, you'll get there.

Remember: becoming a humane leader hinges in part on your ability to manage your energy—and managing your energy starts on Level 1, with the challenge of taking care of your physical energy to feel more pleasure in life. Then you will be able to reclaim back your body and the physical energy that flows through it!

## YOUR HOMEWORK FOR LEVEL 1

How to start putting these learnings into practice, given that most of us are already living complicated lives?

Beginning with this chapter, and in each subsequent chapter describing a level of the human energy field, I'm going to create a space for you—the reader—to experience me as your development adviser. Toward that end, I'm going to give you a homework assignment, just as I did with Emile and others. I'll suggest some key questions to ask yourself and recommend some useful practices. I'll try to keep it simple, since the simpler the questions and practices I recommend, the more likely it is that you'll learn something useful about being intentional in managing your energy.

**Here's an important preamble:** To make these energy shifts happen in you, going forward on all energy levels, I will be constantly asking you to *establish an intention* in everything you undertake. Toward that end, you need to have clear answers to the following three questions first posed by Shakti Gawain:

- Do I desire this intention to happen?
- Do I believe that I can make this intention happen?
- Can I accept the consequences that result from this intention being realized?

At the beginning, shaping intentions through these questions may feel mechanical; that is fine. You may need to build the muscle memory first, to have the right mindset when creating intentionality in everything you do. Once it becomes natural, it will serve as a very powerful tool for helping you be in flow with your energy. At various points, I'll recommend that you jot down some notes in a journal—physical or virtual—so you might want to get ready for that ahead of time.

A key question to ask yourself at Level 1:
Can I be open, curious, and nonjudgmental about what I'm learning about myself?

## SOME INTENTIONS TO SET FOR YOURSELF AT LEVEL 1

### Set the intention to sleep peacefully.

- How many hours do you sleep, on average, on weeknights? Just answer off the top of your head; you don't need to build a spreadsheet.
- Regarding your sleeping hours, what would be your ideal target? Reflect on what happens when you actually hit that target, assuming that you do at least every now and then. How do you feel?

- What gets in the way of hitting your target? Make a list—again, just whatever pops into your head. Now carve out from that list all the things that take energy away from you and decide which of these you can delegate, get rid of entirely, and so on.
- Now *do* it. Shuck that unnecessary stuff. Open new hours in the day to intentionally create space to hit your sleeping target.
- *Don't* fill these new pockets of freedom with more work. If you can't resist this temptation—if carving out time for yourself this way makes you feel guilty or anxious—well, this is *good to know,* as my energy teacher, Linda Caesara, used to tell me. Here's an example of where you need to be both curious and self-compassionate. In the next chapter, we'll work on what gets in the way of your ability to carve out pockets of freedom.

### Set the intention to feel your body when breathing.

We learn to be in and center our bodies through breathing, and proper breathing takes practice. For your homework in this chapter, I include two simple breathing practices. Choose the one that feels right for you.

The first one is called "4–7–8." Close your mouth and quietly inhale through your nose to a mental count of four. Hold your breath for a count of seven. Exhale through your mouth, making a *whoosh* sound for a count of eight. Repeat the process three more times for a total of four breath cycles. Once you've practiced it, notice how you feel before and after you do it. You will likely feel more relaxed and centered as this exercise activates your parasympathetic nervous system.[7] It only takes a few minutes!

The second one I learned from transformational coach Mark Thornton. Focus on your belly a couple of inches below your navel—it helps if you place your hand there—and relax your body. Take shallow "baby" breaths, expanding your belly slowly. As you do, imagine a glowing ball of energy whose glow expands with each breath you take. Stay with this routine for a minute or two. When you're done, bring your attention back to your belly and think about dimming the brightness of the glow.

What do you feel in your body? Take the time to let yourself be curious. Do you feel both more at peace and more energized? If your answer is yes, this is what being centered in your body starts to feel like. If it works for you, try doing it twice a day. Most likely, you'll be surprised at how much energy you can tap into. Accessing your human energy through the physical realm may be easier, and closer, than you think. This was certainly Emile's experience.

I sometimes do this exercise with my clients, especially when I sense at one of our sessions that they are somewhere else and that getting them out of their head and back into their body might be helpful. Many are surprised to find that they respond to it—and it almost always brings them back to the present and the room.

### Set the intention to enjoy your food.

- Do I eat for pleasure? If not, how can I start savoring my food?
- When I start eating, am I grateful for the food at my table?
- Am I aware of the types of food that give me energy? If so, how often do I choose to eat them? If not as often as I would like, why?

- Am I aware of the types of food that take my energy away? If so, how often do I choose to eat them, and why?
- What holds me back from changing my nutrition habits?

Keep in mind that 95 percent of the serotonin in our bodies gets produced in the gut. This is the chemical that carries messages between nerve cells in the brain and throughout our body and plays a key role in your energy level, mood, and sleep patterns. So it's *essential* that we be intentional with our sleeping, breathing, and nutrition habits.

**Set the intention to feel your body
and discover what is holding you back.**

- How do I feel when I'm not able to honor my Level 1 commitments?
- *Connect* to the feeling(s) that arise when you answer that previous question, and ask yourself, *Where in my body do I feel this?* Stay with this feeling; it may take a while before you are able to feel it in your body. Sometimes it helps to name the feeling—as in, *I feel angry,* or sad, or anxious, or whatever.
- Put a hand on the place in your body where you feel the emotion, and ask this part, *What are you protecting?* Stay with the answer that comes to you. Don't question it; just stay with it. Be curious, feel the response, and jot down some journal notes on it. We will use your answers here in our homework in the following chapters.

## THE TAKEAWAYS

❖ Western culture sees mind and body as two separate parts. We need to reclaim a proper balance between mind and body.

❖ The first level of the human energy field is associated with the functioning of our physical body, especially our physical sensations.

❖ Being intentional to feeling your body sensations/ pleasure in everything you do to nourish your body— sleeping, breathing, eating, and so on—is the key.

❖ We center our body through breathing, and proper breathing takes practice.

❖ Many people believe that showing emotions at work is not professional, but when you numb your body for many hours on end, you are likely to lose your ability to feel pleasure.

❖ Feeling your body, being present in your body, is a pre-requisite to gaining access to self—that is, to your unlimited source of human energy.

❖ Feeling sensations in your body is an essential ingredient to help you find where a blocked energy flow is happening in your body.

❖ Energy blockers (trauma) are created in response to the perception of a life-threatening event.

❖ In Western culture, an energy blocker is often patholo-gized as a mental disorder, but many "mental" symp-toms are actually part of the bodily experience.

❖ We have lost sight of the idea that these energy block-ers are an invitation into who we are meant to be. They are a direct through line to gaining access to our unlimited source of energy.

❖ These energy blockers are wounds, which left unattended can cause further harm, but when looked after can help move the body from a state of contraction toward a state of openness.

❖ Managing your energy starts on Level 1 with the challenge of taking care of your physical energy. Learning how to manage your energy at this level will result in amplifying your ability to reclaim your body and feel more pleasure while doing so.

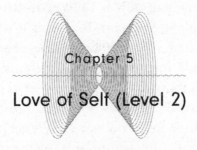

## Chapter 5

# Love of Self (Level 2)

**Y**ou'll recall that in the previous chapter, I introduced Emile—a CEO client—in the context of managing one's physical energy (Level 1: felt sense) and the benefits of mastering that skill. Emile had a powerful, underlying fear of letting people down, which prevented him from setting boundaries to carve out what he called "pockets of personal freedom." Once we surfaced this fear of letting people down, Emile told me enthusiastically that he wanted to explore and resolve it.

I responded affirmatively and encouraged him to *trust the journey* going forward. I told him that, with his permission, I wanted to learn more from his friends and family (to create what I call his personal mirror) and later from his colleagues (to develop his professional mirror) before we drew any conclusions about next steps. He readily agreed and even confessed that he was quite excited to learn what people thought about his energy flow.

My conversation with Emile's family was very revealing and helpful. They are wonderful human beings. They agreed that Emile was very much focused on making things right and making people happy. They were unaware of Emile's determination to carve out some freedom for himself, which didn't surprise me—after all, that might cause them to worry, and he wouldn't want that! When I talked to his colleagues, the same patterns emerged. Again, Emile wanted to make everything *right*. He had very soft boundaries: he was connected and available 24/7. Interestingly, although his ability to make tough people decisions had improved over the years, his colleagues still perceived that as a challenge for him. Again, I wasn't surprised: people who want to please people generally don't look forward to engaging in disciplinary or corrective actions.

This brings us up to our next meeting. I must say, first, that giving feedback to Emile is almost always a pleasure. Usually, he is open and present—all in! This time, though, as the conversation made its way into a difficult zone—how could Emile allow himself some degree of flexibility in terms of "letting people down"?—it got bumpy. I tried several different lines of Socratic questioning, none of which seemed to work. He became fidgety and restless, and I could feel his discomfort. Finally, he verbalized it: "Ricardo, if we continue to have this conversation, it will not go well, because I will never wrap my head around the prospect of letting people down. I've told you—it's just not in my nature!"

As a transformational coach, you have to accept the tough moments and stay as centered as possible—and this was one of the tough ones. Yes, there were other relevant fears and beliefs that Emile and I had to tackle, but by then I had no doubt that, for Emile, the pursuit of interpersonal perfectionism—*pleasing everybody all the time*—was at the heart of what was bugging him. If he could open and explore it, solutions to all of his challenges would flow out of that.

So I paused. I called to mind the wise counsel of one of my former coaches, Jen Cohen, and reminded myself that I was there in full spirit of service *to Emile*. I centered myself, took a deep breath, and leaned forward just as he was pushing backward away from the desk—a two-person choreography of frustration.

"Emile," I said, "I can see that you're getting upset, but let me give it one more try—and if that doesn't work, we'll change topics for today. So please listen to this question with an open mind, if possible. In your role as CEO, is it realistic for you to expect to give everyone in the organization 100 percent of what they need, all of the time?"

He took the question in. He remained silent for a while, seeming to focus intently on the carpet in front of him. When he finally looked up again, I could see that he was troubled. "No," he replied. "That's impossible. One hundred percent is impossible."

"Okay," I said. "So we know the number is not 0 percent. But we also know it's not 100 percent. We know you can't respond to 100 percent of the texts, emails, and voicemails you get. We know you can't sit down and have a chat with 100 percent of the folks who want to walk through your open door. So let's figure out together where you *will* draw the line."

Sounds obvious, right? I wish you could have been in the room. For Emile, hearing me say it out loud was as if some unbearably heavy burden had been lifted from his shoulders. It gave him hope that he might be freed from a relentless treadmill— a path that wasn't allowing him to set boundaries, to create and protect those pockets of freedom, and so on. No, it wasn't the wave of a magic wand; and no, it hasn't been only smooth sailing since then. But starting with that difficult conversation, Emile put himself on a new and productive behavior-shift path within his emotional pattern.

From my point of view, this was good news. By identifying the underlying fear and seeing the irrational outcomes toward which it steered him—the sheer impossibility of pleasing every-body all the time—he now felt that he could start setting some limits and creating some boundaries. With these boundaries would come the freedom to do more of the activities that give him energy—a big step forward. From Emile's perspective, though, he still had that difficult question to address: *Where does this fear of letting people down come from?*

To his credit, he immediately agreed to get back to work on the core question: "*Why* am I so afraid of letting people down? What's the root cause?"

"Great question, Emile," I responded. "Why do you think that is?"

"I don't know," he replied with both amusement and frustration. "I thought maybe *you'd* have a hunch!"

I deflected him. "Well, let's think about it. Remember Level 1? Let's go back again into your body. Let's figure out where in your body you feel this fear of letting people down." I then asked him to close his eyes and remember the last time he let somebody he cared about down. Emile closed his eyes—not before rolling them pointedly!—and gave it a go. To his surprise, he felt it faster this time, and he nodded at me. I then asked him to place his hand where he felt this emotion, and he placed it on his heart.

"Good," I continued. "Now, with your hand on your heart, ask this part of yourself, What is this part protecting?"

To his obvious surprise, Emile made a very interesting response: "This fear is protecting a deeper fear—a fear of being rejected," he said in a flat tone of voice. It was at that moment when, for the first time, Emile was able to feel the part in his body where what I call the "Love of Self gap" existed.

It was a simple session but a very deep one. Toward its end, while still clearly moved by the experience, Emile offered a jumble of interesting observations: "I guess I now know that I've *always* been this way. I've always had this need to *please*. And I've gotten better and better at it over the years—otherwise, I wouldn't be here today—but at the same time,

I was clearly stuck. So now what, Ricardo? I guess the next part of the journey is to focus on closing this Love of Self gap, as you call it, so I can find the freedom of choice to create the boundaries I seek—right?"

Sticking with my Socratic method, I asked him, "What do you feel, Emile?"

"Yes, Ricardo," he exclaimed. "That feels right!"

Obviously, this is an account of a very personal journey.[1] Yours necessarily will be different. But achieving this level of awareness, and connecting to the emotions that come with it, are incredible gateways to closing the Love of Self gap, and accessing the stores of energy—and self-confidence and humane leadership—that are released when that gap is closed.

The second level on our journey is associated with our emotional relationship with ourselves. We need to learn to love and accept ourselves and relate to ourselves in a loving and positive way.[2]

We can't fully access our human energy unless we love ourselves—or, phrased differently, until we are at peace with ourselves. We need to rediscover, forgive, and accept ourselves for who we are before we can tap into the reserves of energy that come with that acceptance and move forward.

When clients reach this stage of the self-discovery journey and I start to make the case for self-love, they typically interrupt me and say something along the lines of, "Hey, whoa, Ricardo—I *do* love myself!"

At which point I tend to ask my irritating question: "I hear you, but do you love yourself 100 percent?"

Well, these are thoughtful people, and they know that almost nothing in real life even approaches 100 percent. Invariably they admit that on the self-love scale, there's some kind of gap between where they are and "100 percent." In most cases, they then start guesstimating how far short of 100 percent they fall.

That's when I let them off the hook. "Whether you love yourself 50 percent or 70 percent is really not the issue," I tell them. "The point is, there's a gap there. And your opportunity lies in *closing* that gap. Every step you take toward closing that gap results in an increased level of self-confidence, which in turn frees up immense amounts of energy." And—I sometimes add—it results in your becoming a more humane and effective leader.

Most of the stuff that holds us back from being able to love ourselves—to being at peace with ourselves—operates on the level of our unconscious and therefore isn't easily accessible. Even when we do manage to get at it rationally, it's not always clear what we should *do* with it. It's like catching some sort of strange new life-form with your bare hands. This is awkward and unaccustomed. My clients and I are problem-solvers, right? And yet, for the most part, we don't know how to *solve* for this.

Eventually, though, most of my clients recognize this energy level as one of the most important and fruitful opportunities for self-development—if only it can be tapped.

So where to start? It turns out that there are many ways to get at closing the Love of Self gap. I'll start with the one that has been most helpful to my clients in connecting and releasing the reserves of energy that have been constrained at this level.

## ENERGY BLOCKERS AND GIVERS

I didn't arrive at these conclusions quickly, or easily. First, I had to experience more of my own life and piece together stories from other people's lives. But somewhere along the line, I began thinking more systematically about this access-to-energy question. Let's assume, I thought to myself, that the abundant energy of a toddler gets blocked by protective strategies created in response to unmet emotional needs. If so, can that process be reversed? As adults, can we get out of these traps and revise, or even let go of, those balancing strategies that we adopted all those years ago? Can we reopen the gates to our human energy by expanding our self-love?

Toward that end, I decided to draw up two lists. One summarizes the relevant emotional layers we've created within ourselves: layers that usually result from being afraid, from feeling overwhelmed, and from seeking to avoid pain. These are the emotions that take us "off-center"—a concept that my sage friend Erica Ariel Fox often talks about, which I'll return to shortly—and get in the way of tapping into our human energy. These are the "energy blockers" that I introduced in the last chapter.

The other list points to what might be called the "energy givers": the emotions that, at least in my experience, give us access to our human energy. And since I ultimately want to wind up this chapter on a happy note—the energy givers—I'll start here with the energy blockers: the emotions that, when they converge, can take us into a behavior pattern that prevents us from accessing our energy.

## LIST ONE: WHAT TAKES ENERGY AWAY?

Everyone is different. Not surprisingly, everybody's list of energy blockers is likely to be somewhat different. I suggest you draw up your own list, perhaps by using the same approach that I did. With a blank document (real or virtual) on the table in front of you, pick an energy-draining emotion—say, anger—and start listing the things that tend to make you angry: I experience anger when . . . Your responses can be super-general or super-specific; however they emerge, though, they should be things that make you move inside, at least a little bit. Don't stop filling the "angry blanks" until you are really feeling the emotion. Then move on to another energy-blocking emotion: frustration, guilt, grief, and so on.

As an example, here are mine.

### Anger

I experience anger when I am not being listened to.

Anger is almost always rooted in insecurity. Bullies at school or in the workplace often come across as angry. They are actually insecure and behave the way they do because lashing out obscures the fact that they're afraid of something.

When anger is not felt by choice, it's an energy blocker. You might ask if it isn't actually an energy door opener, in the sense that when someone gets "hot under the collar," or when the "sparks start to fly," isn't energy being summoned up and released? Well, yes, sort of. But this is energy being channeled into an unproductive end—a destructive emotion.

Some of my clients strongly disagree. They see in anger an emotion that has served to protect them and to makes things happen. Again, this is true up to a certain (limited) point—and only when anger is engaged consciously, by choice. Applied properly, anger can be a great emotional ally for establishing boundaries. But when anger drives things unconsciously, it creates unintended consequences that affect not only your own life but also the lives of those around you.

### Grief

I experience grief when I let people down.

Sooner or later, most of us experience grief—and many of us are surprised at the intensity of that experience, even when the loss has been long expected.

Grief is one of the most important entries on this list, and it's a complicated one. Grief has its own timetable. So what happens when we need to stay in grief but instead try to block it to avoid the pain? This kind of pain avoidance can numb our ability to feel and—if sustained—can reduce access to our source of energy and even lead to depression.

On the other hand: if we lean into the pain that we experience when grieving, it can serve as a healing energy and provide a gateway for personal growth and ultimately enhance our ability to experience joy. The phrase *paralyzed by grief* captures the nadir of the grieving experience. When the paralysis finally starts to ebb, that sets the stage for what eventually may become joy.

Having companions in grief may slow the energy drain associated with loss or may actually accelerate it. Maybe it seems odd to talk about "successful" and "unsuccessful" grieving—but again, most of us have been there. Some companions in grief are healers, but others are not.

## Guilt

I experience guilt when I know I didn't give my best.

Guilt often emerges after anger and fear have been peeled away.

One kind of guilt is essentially circumstantial and external to us—as in, *When I think about the destruction of the environment, I feel a strong sense of guilt.* The other is more directly related to the point of this chapter: *I know what I should have done, and yet I missed doing it. I behaved thoughtlessly, and someone else paid the price.* As we'll see in later chapters, many of the clients I work with are positively riddled with guilt—and some even deny it—which leads to more guilt.

As with grief, there is toxic guilt and healthy guilt. The toxic version is the guilt we do nothing about. The healthy form of guilt serves as an engine—motivating us to solve the problem, learn from it, and never do it again.

All of these are what might be called "low-level" emotions, and they've been studied in depth by neuroscientists. Guilt consistently shows up as the emotion closest to the one at the very bottom of the pack—shame—which I turn to next.

## Shame

I experience shame when I fall short of following my principles.

What is shame? According to the dictionary, it's the feeling of distress that arises when you're aware that your behavior has been wrong or foolish. According to University of Houston professor Brené Brown, guilt is focused on behavior ("I did something bad"), while shame focuses on yourself ("I am bad"). Guilt would lead you to say, "I'm sorry I made a mistake," while shame would lead you to say, "I'm sorry I *am* a mistake."

Shame is one of the most powerful energy blockers. Almost everyone has some profound insecurity as a result of "being bad"—something that they're ashamed of and that they fear will be found out. Try this energy experiment: Think about your deepest insecurity—the thing that you're most ashamed of. As you do, monitor what you're feeling. Is "energy blocking" a reasonable description? Shame leads to secrets, and secrets can take us away from holding our own truth, and every time you move away from your truth, you block access to your human energy.

One interesting truth is that shame is self-inflicted. The trick here is figuring out how to dig ourselves out of the "shame hole" and escape from this paralyzing emotion as swiftly as possible.

This is not to suggest that shame isn't real or deeply felt or that it's easy to solve and move away from. It's rarely that simple. But there are well-trodden paths that we can follow to get out of these thickets—and we have every reason to try to do so.

The list above certainly isn't a comprehensive set of energy blockers—it's simply my list. Others might include jealousy, envy, apathy, and so on. Once you've come up with your own list of energy blockers, take some time to reflect on it. Did you feel it when you were writing it? (I hope so.) Let yourself be even more curious. For example, where in your body did you feel these emotions? If you felt the blocking emotions in different parts of your body, do you see patterns in that? Are you curious about why you listed the negative emotions in the order that you did? Are you surprised by the ways you completed the partial sentences? How difficult was it for you to connect to these emotions?

## LIST TWO: WHAT GIVES US ACCESS?

I won't spend as much time on this second list. That's not because it's less important—in fact, it's very important because it will remind you to spend time every day doing things that will help give you access to your human energy. But for now, I'll keep it simple. Make your own second list, following the steps outlined above. What emotional states give you enhanced access to your human energy—that is, serve as energy givers? Here are several that I wrote down.

### Gratitude

I experience gratitude when someone gives expecting nothing in return.

Recently my firm hosted a virtual global gathering of some one thousand colleagues. I was asked, on very short notice, to reach out to a high-profile CEO to see if she would record an inspirational video to be shown at the gathering. Would she be willing to share her personal experience of the work that we've done together—how it has affected her personally and professionally—while at the same time challenge us to keep growing in the field of developing humane leaders?

As I said, this came to me on short notice. I knew very well how busy she was. So, with some reluctance, I reached out to her—only to find that she was scheduled to leave for a vacation in two days. Mission impossible! I sat down to figure out who I could call next. But even before I had many names written down, I got an email from her chief of staff, with a video attached.

I watched it, and it was exactly what we were looking for. I was blown away and filled with deep gratitude. Yes, it was a kick-ass video: emotional, inspiring, and challenging. But what *really* moved me to tears was that she had dropped everything she was doing to help out her coach. She had my back, and boy, was I grateful!

Whenever I find my spirits flagging, I remind myself of this story of generosity and others like it—and my spirits immediately lift. There is great energy generated, stored, and shared in gratitude.

What are you grateful for? What's the most special thing that life has given you, after life itself? When life takes you by surprise and forces a little wonderment on you, what is it that you're finding wondrous?

I said "a little wonderment" purposefully. Gratitude may be contained, but it is still powerful and durable. "Gratitude is a divine emotion," wrote Charlotte Brontë. "It fills the heart, but not to bursting; it warms it, but not to fever."

Personally, I am deeply grateful that I am alive and have my wife, Paty, and my children, Diana, Ricky, and Andy, in my life. Every time I think of them—as I often do during my morning meditation—it lifts my spirits, no matter how hard my day is likely to be.

## Bliss

I experience bliss when listening to music that takes me back to my youth.

Bliss is that rare state of perfect happiness that puts you in a space where you forget about everything else. I'm sure that this is the emotion that many of us felt when we were cradled by our mothers for the very first time.

Again, we arrived in this world with our hearts completely full and our minds completely empty. This is part of the reason why we feel such peace when we are able to silence our minds. With practice, it can connect us to a state of grace that we long to get back to, on the most fundamental of levels. Sometimes people describe this as a healing state—a sort of therapeutic respite. That's true enough, but it stops short of the full story. When we silence our minds, we start to open the door that fear closed, all those years ago.

Bliss is where we came from. When we get a taste of it in later life, we want that experience to stay with us as long as it can. We want to sample and savor that energy. Some types of music immediately take me there. So does a spectacular sunset while walking on the beach. What about you? What is your gateway to bliss, around all the complexities of life? What gives you immediate access?

## Love

I experience love when I am hugged, unprompted, by the people I care about.

When I drew up this list, I didn't put love at the top. Afterward, I wondered about that. Shouldn't love have come first? All you need is love, as the Beatles put it, and that's not far off the mark. Our ability to love ourselves and others largely determines whether we will be able to tap into our human energy. When we are in a positive state of love with ourselves, we are at our best. We own our voice, and we step forward with confidence into whatever we set our minds and hearts to. When we are in love with the members of our closest inner circle—our family and friends—we feel protected, safe, and invincible. When we are in love with our colleagues at work, we become generous with one another without expecting anything back. When we are in love with humanity, our purpose flourishes and we become inspired to give back and to pay it forward.

So yes, nothing yields and rewards human energy like love. The transfer of energy depends on connectedness, in one way or another. We *are* love. Love is a connecting energy, it's the ultimate healing energy, and as humans, we have the innate need to belong. When I'm in love, I'm connected to the source. I'm connected to my creative power.

So why didn't love top my list? Because it is not easy to be in love. It's not easy to love ourselves and to stay in love with others. And because it's such a powerful emotion, it cuts both ways. Moving out of love takes significant energy away. It's so painful, in fact, that we immediately take steps to stop the process—sometimes at all costs. And that's when we resolve (consciously or unconsciously) to avoid feeling that pain ever again.

Think of all of those thousands of pop tunes that are the counterpoint—the flip side—of *all you need is love*. Think of all the harm that is done by people who seek love but can't find it.

But reflections on love can't end on that sad note! There is no surer access to our internal energy than love. Love is worth every pain that we experience in order to earn it.

## CENTERING YOUR EMOTIONAL DIMENSION

I hope that by this point you have a reasonable sense of what I mean by energy blockers and energy givers. I hope you have at least an incipient sense of what's on your two lists, which will be different from mine and everyone else's. Certainly, each of my clients' lists is different. Even more interesting, many feel their emotions in different places in their body than I do.

This realization leads me to look at some of these same ideas in three different dimensions of human energy: the physical (Level 1), the emotional (Levels 2 and 4), and the mental (Level 3). We will learn about Levels 3 and 4 in the following chapters. It's within these three dimensions that we become (or fail to become) adept at centering ourselves. *Centering* is a common verb in therapeutic contexts, which means that it tends to take on lots of different meanings. For now, think of it as simply meaning "getting things in balance."

Getting things in balance—centering ourselves—in each of these dimensions gives us increased access to our human energy. By centering all three of these dimensions, we gain access to self—our essential being, which distinguishes us from others—and experience a higher level of access to our human energy. The more we are able to connect to this space within us, the more energized we feel throughout our lives.

We reconnect with our inner toddler. We feel free!

We'll start here with the emotional dimension because many people find this to be the most challenging. Think back to all the low-energy emotions we just discussed—things like guilt and anger. We can center our emotional dimension by gathering up all these low-energy emotions and countering them with self-acceptance.

We do so by undertaking a journey of self-discovery. We need to learn who we truly are. In other words, what would our personality be without interference from our self-limiting fears and beliefs? This journey, which constitutes the core of experiencing human energy, is far from easy. But closing the gaps can be profoundly liberating and energizing.

Centering yourself in the emotional dimension has many facets. Think back to the discussions of pain and fear in earlier chapters. Part of the journey is to bring those pains and fears out into the open—into the realm of consciousness—and accept them. By this, I don't mean we should accept them as a given, as something that is immutable and unchangeable. Far from it! Instead, I mean, *we should accept them as a part of our personal history*, which we are now in the process of amending. We are getting away from the narrative that fenced us in and cut us off from our human energy. We are accepting a new self that is capable of self-love—and therefore has the enormous benefit of self-confidence and vastly increased freedom of choice.

So how do we center our emotional dimension?

We center our emotions with *love of self*. Most of us don't love ourselves nearly enough, and we need to get better at it. But again, for most of us, that's easier said than done. So let's dig deeper by looking again at the Love of Self gap. Uncovering, and then closing, the Love of Self gap are challenges that are inextricably tied up with our fears, as explained in earlier chapters. And with the vast majority of my clients, when I ask them what they're afraid of, their response is, *I'm afraid to fail*.

This is true no matter how successful they are. When I probe, I also find that very few of them ever speak about the fear of failure openly—which is understandable but still unfortunate. Many would derive great benefit and comfort if they were to discover that they are not alone in this fearful state. They have no real understanding of all the unintended and negative consequences that grow out of this state—and, conversely, how much energy they would unlock if they could only let it go.

The fear of failure is a symptom of the larger fear system. Below this fear, we can find deeper fears and deeper levels of insecurity. Every one of my clients' cases is different, of course, but for our purposes here, the common thread is a *lack of self-love*. So—as was the case with Emile—I almost always arrive at the point of asking that crucial question: On a scale of 1 to 10, how would you rate your love of self? Do you love yourself 100 percent?

Maybe that sounds like an odd question. Think of it this way: to be 100 percent self-assured with a healthy ego, your level of self-love needs to be reasonably close to 100 percent— in other words, no dark recesses of submerged self-loathing allowed. To this day, I have yet to find a human who loves himself or herself this much. I am certainly not there! So, really, part of our journey is about learning to love ourselves a little bit more, inch by inch, as much as we can—because any space of self that is left unloved gives room to insecurity. It amplifies the voice of the Critic, nipping at our heels like a border collie: *Don't screw up!* Superheroes don't even need to be told; they just strap on that obligation and struggle and suffer.

When we get this deep in a session, I try to steer clients toward a memory of a time when they needed to be loved and, for whatever reason, that love wasn't available to them. Whenever this happened, we sought to stay safe, leading us to blame ourselves for the situation. Why? Imagine how unsafe we would have felt back then if we had recognized that our caretakers were unable to give us what we longed for and desired from them. Unacceptable! So the moment we started to blame ourselves—to unconsciously feel safer—was the moment that we started to feel less lovable.

Again, this is the Love of Self gap.

Let's look at another example of discovering and closing the Love of Self gap: this time featuring an EVP and executive committee member in a Fortune 100 company. I'll call her Katie.

After a certain amount of reluctant exploration, Katie finally told me that she only got recognition from her mom when she brought home a report card with straight As. Then the inevitable happened: she got her first B. She told me she was terrified when she contemplated showing that flawed report card to her mother. So she didn't. She hid it as best as she could.

But of course that wasn't the end of the story. Even now I can see her looking out her office window, drifting off into the past, recollecting. Thinking out loud, she remembered, before mom found out, she made sure to double down on her school work. The Critic stepped forward and demanded perfection: not only at school but also at home. The young Katie started doing yard work and house work without being asked. (Her mother was understandably confused by these developments.) *Be proactive*, the voice told her, *because if you're not, you're going to be back in that same terrible spot*. She actually made a reference to "the voice," which was not a phrase we had used up to that point.

Somewhere toward the end of that story, she began to refocus on the room she was in and the person she was with (me). She told me that the voice was still with her, pushing her to do whatever it took to *stay out of trouble* and to get the recognition that she craved!

I waited a few beats, and then I told her there was no particular reason to get rid of the voice. She looked surprised, and I think a little relieved. (As I said earlier, many of us believe that it's the voice that actually pushes open the doors to our successes.) But, I continued, *it seems like it might be a good idea to give that voice a new job.*

Again, this wasn't an original insight on my part. I came across it at Dick Schwartz's Internal Family Systems training, introduced in chapter 3. To recap briefly here: Dick observes that many psychotherapeutic frameworks have focused on the idea of *getting rid of the Critic* (in my terminology). "Let's *not* get rid of the Critic," Dick Schwartz says, in so many words. "It has served you well. Let's honor it, thank it, and help it take on a new job."

And that's what I said to my client. Let's give the Critic the new job of *cheering* for you and helping you believe in yourself. Let's help the Critic understand that it can become the Cheerleader because it sees that you are no longer so young and vulnerable. Let's take one more step toward loving yourself a bit more.

Tears were shed, as I recall.

## IF YOU NEED AN ALLY, FIND ONE

Roughly one out of every two of my clients finds themselves getting stuck, at one point or another. For them, and maybe for you, I have some further thoughts.

First of all, you're already in an amazing place—far different from where you were before. You're exploring your own story, with the intention of getting to the root causes of things and engaging in some healing.

Second, it's very likely that your story—while unique—fits into a bigger picture. Again, most of our fears grow out of some hurt or pain that we experienced in our past, at a time when we needed to be loved and that need was not met. That probably wasn't our caregivers' fault—chances are that they were doing the best they knew how to do—but it certainly wasn't *our* fault. After all, we were emotionally dependent and relatively powerless. But out of love for our caregivers, we chose not to blame them. The inevitable result? We blamed ourselves. Like Emile, we decided that, for whatever reason, we were not sufficiently "lovable"—at which point, our self-acceptance gap cracked open and began to grow. Our insecurities grew along with it, and our balancing systems kicked in to compensate.

I assume you're following this logic, and you're thinking to yourself, "Thanks, Ricardo, but I'm still *stuck*. How do I get unstuck?"

This is the point on my clients' self-discovery journeys when I often do a reality check on them, and on myself. Someone who is *truly stuck* may be in that state for a really good reason, most likely trauma. That is a line that I don't step over, so I am very likely at that point to recommend that my client "find an ally"—by which I mean, *get expert help.* My experience doesn't qualify me to provide that help, but it qualifies me to suggest what kind of therapeutic support might be most helpful and to lend whatever help I can, with an eye on the journey that is to follow.

If you can get to the root cause of your self-love gap on your own, through deep personal introspection, good for you! Embrace your success, and think of it as your apprenticeship moment in a discipline that you will practice from here on out. But if after many rounds of knocking on the door you keep arriving at "I don't know," I highly recommend finding an ally who can guide you through what is likely to be a highly emotional and fruitful journey.

There are great resources out there. Maybe you'd like to start by reading how some smart potential allies think about these issues. I find the late Bert Hellinger's work on Family Constellations and Dick Schwartz's concept of Internal Family

Systems particularly efficient and effective in unlocking and placing emotional energy in order to reduce the self-love gap.[3] Or maybe you (or your company) can arrange a consultation with experts.

Again, allies are out there. The network of consultants within the Mobius Executive Leadership firm, for example, is second to none.[4] I've worked closely with many of them, and together we've unlocked immense emotional energy related to self-acceptance.

Keep in mind that unlocking energy at Level 2 is likely to be a very emotional experience. In order to experience the joy that comes from managing energy at this level, many of us—even most of us—first have to go through grief. As stated before, grief can serve as the gateway to joy. In many cases, it's through grief that our walls fall down and allow us access and reconnection to higher levels of self-love.

If and when grief comes, *lean into it.* That's probably your best way to cleanse what is holding you back. If this is how it plays out for you, be prepared to go through a couple of boxes of tissues. Have faith. Let go. Again, you're on the right path, and you are definitely moving in the right direction.

## YOUR HOMEWORK FOR LEVEL 2

One more time: as stated in the previous chapter, the intention of the "your homework" section is to create space for you to experience me as your development adviser. I'll offer the same *very important* preamble: to make these energy shifts happen in you, you need to *set an intention* in everything you desire—which in this chapter means closing the Love of Self gap. And once again, make sure you have clear answers to my three questions:

- Do I desire this intention to happen?
- Do I believe that I can make this intention happen?
- Can I accept the consequences that result from this intention being realized?

A key question to ask yourself at Level 2:

I'll restate the question I asked at Level 1: Can I be open, curious, and nonjudgmental about what I'm learning about myself?

## SOME INTENTIONS TO SET FOR YOURSELF AT LEVEL 2

### Set the intention for growth in love of self.

- Do you love yourself 100 percent? Here and now, you need to speak truth to yourself. It's important. If you find it easier, rate yourself on a scale of 1 to 10, with 1 being you really don't love yourself and 10 being you really do. So how much do you love yourself?
- Okay now, *why?* Why did you come up with the answer you did? Stick with this question. Take the time to journal all the answers that come to you, even if they seem trivial. (They may not be.)
- Based on past experience, I'll guess that you didn't give yourself a 10. Well, it's helpful to know when we're living with a Love of Self gap. Discovering and accepting that fact gives us energy to find ways to grow the love within.
- Like physical health, love of self is essential to managing our energy. So how do we cultivate it? Try the following:

**Cultivate emotional awareness.** Find a quiet room where you can go within yourself without any interruption. (Leave your mobile outside!) Feel your emotions. What takes your energy away? What makes you feel anger, grief, guilt, shame, and so on? Create a list of your own, like the one I described earlier in the chapter. It may help to open each entry with: *I experience [anger, grief, guilt, and so on] when . . .* and complete that entry until you finish. Think about how you feel after doing this exercise.

Now do the same exercise focused on the question: What gives you energy? What makes you feel grateful, joyous, loving, and so on? Again, create a list of your own, using the steps listed above. At the end, ask yourself how you feel after connecting with what gives you energy. Also consider asking people who know you well if they see something on the list that surprises them or if they would add anything to the list.

What if you aren't able to make contact with your emotions? Again, this is a good thing to know. Perhaps your body is numbed, which is why doing your homework in the previous chapter is essential. Your physical body needs to intentionally find the way back to feeling pleasure again. If still you are not able to feel emotions in your body, then find an ally, as described earlier in this chapter. Meanwhile, keep reading!

**Create your emotional body map.** Read your energy-taking list out loud. Visualize it, feel it, *get into it*! Do it one emotion at a time. Let's say you start with anger. Start reading and feeling. By the time you're done, I'm betting, you will be *pissed off*. Well, good! Stay with that emotion and ask yourself, *Where in my body do I feel anger?* Place a hand on the part of your body where you feel angry. Now take a piece of paper, draw a body—great art not needed here—and draw a symbol that represents anger for you on the part of your body where you feel it. Repeat the same steps for grief, guilt, and so on. Now repeat this mapping exercise using your energy-giving list and drawing on the same map. Be creative. Use colors that mean something to you. It's *your* map.

A word of caution: opening the doors to your deepest emotions can be charged terrain. So, when exploring, it may help to do the mapping as if you were a journalist observing your own mind.

Once you have the completed map, study it. Try to be curious and open to what it may teach you. If your map is like mine, and those that my clients have created over the years, you will be surprised to discover how different emotions live in different parts of your body.

**Discover your original wound (the root cause).** Energy follows energy. *Follow the energy of your energy-taking emotions* because they are wisdom teachers. How is this done? Try these steps . . .

Retrace the learnings from your emotional body map. For example: Place your hand where you draw grief in your body, visualize what takes you there, and stay there until you feel sad. When connected emotionally to this place in your body, ask yourself what you're afraid of. Write the answer(s) in your journal. For Emile, as you'll remember, it was the fear of letting people down.

Once you've identified your fear, ask what the *root cause* of this fear is. In other words, you need to go a layer deeper. When you ask this question, it may help to keep your eyes closed. For Emile, you'll recall, the root cause—the original wound—was the fear of being rejected and abandoned.

When you push on these kinds of questions, you are knocking on the door that separates your conscious and unconscious minds. Use the opportunity to connect with your past and to explore what you find there. Most likely, you will make discoveries from long ago. As I explained in chapter 2, our emotional patterns—including our fears—are mostly created very early in our lives, and you may need to go back there.

Maybe half of my clients make deep and meaningful connections to their past, which provide deep answers to the questions on the table. The other half either doubt what they discover or simply get stuck at "I don't know." If you arrive at this impasse, try not to get frustrated. Knock on that door some more and then some more. Honor this situation as an opportunity to learn more about yourself.

And once again: if you get stuck in this effort to discover your root cause, you may want to enlist an ally to help out.

**Set the intention to heal and integrate your root cause.**

- Assuming that you ultimately come up with your root cause, you'll now want to work on healing and integrating it. Here I'd recommend partnering with an expert in integrating body, mind, and spiritual energy. As I've already shared, Internal Family Systems practitioners do great work in this arena.
- The bottom line: discovering, healing, and integrating the original root cause is one of the most effective ways that I have experienced in intentionally growing Love of Self energy.

## THE TAKEAWAYS

❖ We need to learn to love and accept ourselves as we are and relate to ourselves in a loving and positive way to gain access to our energy.

❖ Most of us have a gap between the ideal level of self-love (100 percent) and our current level. Every step we take toward closing that gap results in an increased level of self-confidence, which in turn frees up immense amounts of energy.

❖ There are emotions that take energy away and emotions that connect us deeper within our energy. These emotions complement each other: grief is a gateway to joy and joy is a gateway to amplifying love of self.

❖ Early in our lives, when we needed to be loved and our need was not met, to stay safe we chose to believe that we were not sufficiently "lovable"—at which point, our self-acceptance gap cracked open, and our insecurities began to grow.

❖ When our insecurities grow, our balancing systems kick in to compensate.

❖ Moving unconscious emotions to consciousness is key to growing our love of self. If you get stuck, find an ally—which may mean seeking professional help. Always remember: *there's no shame attached.*

❖ All of us have a Love of Self gap—but love is worth every pain we experience to earn it.

# Chapter 6

# Clarity of Thought (Level 3)

Helen is the regional head of a $10 billion globe-spanning consumer health-products company. When it comes to searching out new models for growth and partnering with colleagues across the business to make things happen, she is second to none. For all these reasons and more, Helen is respected by people throughout the organization and is seriously being considered as CEO-successor material.

When we first began talking, though, there clearly was one major challenge that Helen had to face. Even though she loved most aspects of her job, every time that she had to make a tough people decision—which happened regularly in her leadership position—she experienced high levels of anxiety, especially if the decision involved someone she cared about. She constantly heard a voice in her head telling her, *You should give John another chance! Perhaps if you had been closer to him, this would have never happened! How will he be able to support his family?*—and so on, and so on. By her own account, she would "flee," dragging her feet for months, delaying the outcome that most people could see was coming. And all the while, she knew in her heart that John's departure was inevitable and that it would be the right thing for both John and the organization. And although ultimately Helen would make things happen, her procrastination only caused more grief for the people involved in the process—and absolutely consumed her in the meantime.

Helen had no idea about how to address this problem. It wasn't for lack of trying. For example, she had hired a succession of executive coaches, which for a variety of reasons hadn't worked out very well.

In truth, I found helping Helen a bit tricky at first; she is very selective when it comes to confiding in people. Second, she was understandably skeptical of coaches. But we met and talked, and as I slowly earned her trust, she started to open up. For example, I learned what gives her energy and what takes energy away from her. But every time that we tried to explore what was going on within her and discover what was holding her back, we hit a wall. She was clearly uncomfortable every time that I tried to focus our conversations on *her*—a difficult subject for us to avoid!

Time passed, and one day, we made an unexpected breakthrough: Helen mentioned in passing how guilty she felt about all the time we were spending focusing on her and her issues.

This was a compelling emotional clue that I immediately picked up on. "Why would you feel guilty about *that*?" I asked her.

She paused, seemingly lost in thought, and finally responded. "I just remembered something," she said. "Something that my mother told me, many years ago—that taking care of ourselves is selfish and that we are put in this world to take care of others."

Bingo! In other words, unlike many of my clients, Helen wasn't afraid to explore within herself. But she believed that this kind of internal focus amounted to being selfish. So I asked her how she would feel subscribing to a *new* belief, along the lines of "To take better care of others, first take better care of yourself."

*Not* bingo! Based on the expression that settled on her face, she thought I was suggesting that she do something *horrible*. But I was ready to take that heat. I took a deep breath, audibly, and allowed a minute of silence to go by. Then I asked *her* to take a deep breath, close her eyes, and to describe why she was so upset with me for making that fairly innocuous suggestion.

Eventually, after a few minutes of deep breathing and calming down, she said, "If I did what you asked, I would be betraying my mom."

Then she began crying silently.

No, Helen wasn't afraid to explore within and do personal work, but a blind loyalty to a long-ago directive was holding her back and preventing her from continuing her journey forward, personally and professionally. I let her grieve for a few minutes—as noted in the last chapter, grief can provide a very powerful healing energy—and once I felt she was okay to go forward, I asked her again if she'd be willing to "try on for size" a new belief.

She nodded, almost imperceptibly. It's amazing how quickly we can make progress when we are *ready* to make progress.

"And assuming we could figure out a way to make it work, what would you like this new belief to be?"

"Something along the lines of what you said," she replied. Her paraphrase was far better than my own first stab. "Taking care of myself is not selfish; it is an act of generosity to others. By taking care of myself first, I can take better care of my family and my team and contribute more to society."

Back to bingo! It was a super-inspiring moment, and from that moment on, Helen's work on herself accelerated, and today, she balances tough people decisions (at home and at work) on a timely basis, with rigor and care.

We met again recently. We talked about the benefits of what I refer to as "updating your belief system"—that is, bringing the whole backlog of thoughts and directives that we carry with us into conformance with today's reality. She agreed with that description and affirmed that her clarity of thought had been amplified significantly. For example, she said, nowadays when she needs to have a difficult conversation, it's far clearer to whom she has to talk, and how soon, and exactly what needs to be discussed. In fact, she continued, these conversations are now happening *proactively*—not being shied away from—and as a result, her leadership team is more supportive of her than ever before.

She laughed at that point. "Maybe it's a coincidence," she said, "but the way things are flowing now, we don't seem to need as many difficult conversations!"

The third level within the human energy field focuses on our mental activity and the sense of clarity that results when that activity is free from emotional obstacles.

Developing the self-love described in the last chapter is aimed in part at helping us trust our instincts more. When we have the benefit of more self-confidence, we turn more readily to our intuition. Then the challenge becomes to bring that intuition together with clarity of thought—and when that happens, we unlock great reserves of human energy. And when *that* happens, we are free to become more humane leaders.

"Clarity of thought" is a concept that's a little hard to capture in words, but let me offer some examples. What does "clear thinking" look like?

Think of those fight scenes in the latest Sherlock Holmes movies, in which Robert Downey Jr.'s Holmes slows down the action to about one-seventh speed and narrates it for our benefit: First, I'm going to do this. And now this. And now this. Ah, if real life were only like that!

Well, there *are* some real-world equivalents. I'm thinking of the interviewee who gets asked a complicated, multipart question and says in response, "Well, let me say five things about that"—and then proceeds to say five trenchant, on-point things.

My reaction to that kind of mastery is fourfold:

1. Wonderful!
2. I bet she got a good night's sleep last night (Level 1).
3. Looks like she's confident and at peace with herself (Level 2).
4. I bet she's in mental flow (Level 3)!

Managing your energy at Level 3 enables you to understand the circumstances in which you find yourself in clear ways, both linear and nonlinear. Again, it enables a harmonious and complementary blend of rationality and intuition. Your creative energy will encounter less friction and will have fewer distracting thoughts to deal with. Why? Because you will feel less of a need to replay the past. And because you won't always feel compelled to *do more* in the present. (Sometimes trying to "do more" is a waste of time and energy.) And finally because you won't feel as much of a need to control the future. All of this adds up to enhancing your ability to be present in the moment and having more faith in your own ability and the ability of others to solve complex problems on the spot, in real time.

What does this mean in practical terms? Well, it keeps you out of traps like overpreparing for a meeting, trying to anticipate things that simply can't be anticipated. It helps you to *be here now* at that meeting—present, spontaneous, and firing on all cylinders. Think about a regularly scheduled meeting that you attend with more or less the same cast of characters every time. Do the really interesting observations tend to come from the same people, meeting after meeting? And are those people the relatively high-energy participants at the table? Think of those people in terms of Levels 1 and 2, and in terms of my four bullet points above. Do you see how these complementary layers begin to create what might be called an Effective Zone—and position you to succeed in that zone?

My clients say that when they get into the Effective Zone, they feel *great*. I recently heard from one of my clients who was thriving in his position as CEO: "It feels as if things just *appear* to you, and solutions just roll out of your mind." It's clear to me, just from hearing these kinds of reports, that there aren't a lot of things that are *more* energizing, at least in the office setting. And by the way: the people around you tend to notice and tend to be grateful. It's nice to have an energetic and decisive problem-solver in the room, right?

So that's the good news. But like all steps along the path of energy management, this one is easier talked about than taken. I've already mentioned the need to be physically and emotionally balanced as a prerequisite to unlocking higher clarity of thought. There's another factor at work here, as well. At Level 2—discussed in the previous chapter—we encountered the first of two internal balancing systems: the fear system, including a constellation of fears ultimately created with the intention of protecting you from experiencing pain or getting hurt again, and the belief system.

## UPDATING YOUR BELIEF SYSTEM

The belief system is our internal rule book, which combines two kinds of beliefs. The first is all that stuff that is implanted in our minds—with the best of intentions—by our parents, caretakers, other family members, and the society around us. "Take care of others first," Helen's mother told her, all those years ago. "Men don't cry," my father told me. "Better to be the head of a mouse than the tail of a lion," my Mexican culture told me. These things add up and—with repetition—

serve as powerful constraints on the way that we think and behave.

The second type of beliefs are all those deals we cut with ourselves—those self-inflicted strictures that we imposed on ourselves in very uncomfortable moments in our life and that have stuck with us ever since, like barnacles on the hidden hull of a ship. These deals of self-accommodation impede the free flow of our thoughts, just as barnacles cause ships to drag in the water and burn more fuel.[1]

Obviously, these two streams intersect and overlap. The first kind of rule gets introduced at a time in our lives when our ability to discern is either nonexistent or severely limited. We place our full, blind faith in our parents and other caregivers because we trust them, or we have no choice—and so they succeed in instilling in us their beliefs, many of which have been passed on from generation to generation. Of course, some of those beliefs represent hard-won wisdom and should be treasured. For example, I like "Leaves of three, let it be"—sound advice for avoiding poison ivy and poison oak—but there are other bits of "wisdom" that are outmoded or flat-out wrong. And so we take in all kinds of guidance, good and bad, and let that vast storehouse of submerged rules guide our thinking for years or decades and to this day continue to guide unconsciously the way we see and act in the world.

As for the second kind of beliefs, we go about the burdensome task of negotiating an endless collection of small contracts with ourselves. Some are mundane and relatively harmless. Others are far more subtle and insidious. Sometimes we cut these deals without even knowing it; other times, we forget that we created this distorted rule that we subsequently internalized. As we grow older, we take ownership of the unconscious pen that wrote our rule book—and as we experience new life discomforts, we add new rules.

Like the fear system, our belief system is also a protective mechanism, intended to keep us on the lookout and thereby buffer us from the hard knocks of our lives. It compounds the insulating effect of the fear system. Just to complicate things further, these two balancing systems overlap with each other. Sometimes the fear system steps in and censors certain kinds of thoughts, and sometimes the belief system messes around with our emotions. In addition, even though we were raised to conquer our fears, it's very unlikely that we also were raised to challenge our parents' belief system. After all, they gave it to us with good intentions in the belief that it would serve us as well as it served them.

No wonder, then, that it's so difficult for us to look inside ourselves to find the answers we seek.

Not all beliefs are given to us in early childhood. Here I'll share a personal story about the type of beliefs that we sometimes acquire later in life. Back when I was in my early twenties, I experienced what felt like an almost existential threat—one that caused me to add a belief in my rule book: *Be damned careful when you take a risk!*

Let me set the stage. I'm in a room with a panel of professors in front of me, all of them prepared and inclined to make me sweat a bit. Behind me is my entire family. And I do mean my *entire* family: parents, siblings, aunts, grandparents, girlfriend, and more were there. This was the day of my professional exam—a rite of passage during which you were challenged on your thesis, and you either did or didn't pass. I was feeling quite confident—in fact, *too* confident, as one of the professors later told me: confident to the point of appearing arrogant.

It was all going fine until one of the professors asked me to explain one of the formulas used in the calculation of the break-even point of the business under discussion. And at that point, my mind went totally blank. I wasn't able to answer. I could barely talk. Just putting this long-ago memory to paper is making me sweat!

Well, once that professor smelled blood, he didn't let go. He made me *suffer* from that moment forward, adding salt to the wound, insult to injury, even threatening to flunk me, in front of all my family. I felt so ashamed. Finally, when the ordeal was over, I was asked to leave the room, along with my family, so my professors could deliberate on my final grade.

Picture us all outside in the hallway. You could have heard a pin drop. I couldn't look my parents in the eye. Eventually the door opened, and I was asked to come back in by myself. And for the first several minutes, it was just about as bad as it could be. The professor who had been chasing me down the road ranted—really *ranted*—about how I was an embarrassment to the university and that he disagreed with the majority of the panel and that therefore he wanted no further part of this. He scooped up his papers and stalked out of the room, almost violently.

I was still confused. Disagreed *how*? With what? At that point, one of the other professors looked at me with a smile and congratulated me on passing my exam.

Even though my family was thrilled, and even though we had the obligatory celebration, I enjoyed none of it. I felt then, and for quite a long time afterward, that I was damaged goods—a failure. In so many words, I made a promise to myself: *Never, ever again will I suffer such a humiliation.* And, as an extension: *From now on, I will overprepare for everything, so that I'll never again risk failing!*

Here's the point: this new belief in my rule book stuck with me for many, many years. From that moment on, I overprepared for everything. I pushed myself to ensure that everything I delivered, at work and at home, would be flawless. And guess what? For years, it seemed to work. Every year, more or less on schedule, I got promoted, and the feedback I received was always similar: "Ricardo is a super-reliable colleague."

It worked—that is, until I started to get closer to the top of the house at my first employer, Citigroup. At that point, the feedback took a new and unexpected turn—and again, it was consistent: "Ricardo is solid at making things happen, but he is risk averse, and he won't grow until he learns to trust his intuition more and take more risks." Uh-oh!

I still remember hearing this feedback from Jose Tosi, then the CEO of Citigroup Mexico. At the beginning of our talk, I told him that his feedback made me feel like a failure. He looked at me with a smile and said, "Good! That is exactly what I wanted you to feel. You need to learn how to feel comfortable when failing. That's where your growing edge is. Getting out of your comfort zone is what's going to help you stretch yourself and grow. In fact, Ricardo, if you're not consistently failing 30 percent of the time—three out of ten—then you're not trying hard enough."

Ouch! His words hit me like a bucketful of cold water. And into my mind—I kid you not—flashed an image of that woeful graduation party and the moment when I first promised myself that I would never fail again. And now, in real time, in Jose Tosi's office, I realized that that long-ago resolution was not only not serving me anymore, but it had turned into a self-limiting belief.

I thanked him for his insight and candor and told him honestly that I was determined to make the most of this conversation. No, change didn't come overnight. In fact, my "intellectual muscle memory" betrayed me quite often, but I worked at it. I searched out and tried hard to connect with my intuitive power. Eventually, I gained a reputation for being quite a risk-taker—a far cry from that shaken young man at that graduation party. With Jose's bucket of cold water kicking off the process, I was able to identify my self-limiting belief, soften it, and ultimately let it go to become a better leader. It was okay to fail. Where before I saw challenges, I now saw more possibilities. A year later I started my MBA, got promoted, and got engaged. Thank you, Jose!

Of course, that wasn't the only transition I had to make. Still lurking back there were all those antique words of wisdom passed on by my family, community, and culture.

I've already told you that my father used to play down emotions whenever he saw my eyes welling up. His guidance began and ended with those three short words: *Men don't cry.*

But that's not where it stopped. Not only did I accept that at face value, I later added my own subclauses to his observation: "Men who cry are weak" and—even worse—"Vulnerability is weakness."

I was now on a slippery slope. As a result of my grandfather's and (later on) my father's belief system, as well as my own interpretations on the theme, I significantly reduced my ability to connect emotionally with myself and others. And even that wasn't the end of it. Somewhere along the line, my belief system acquired another extension of the theme: it's unprofessional to show emotions at work. Whenever you start feeling strong emotions in the workplace—especially "negative" emotions like sadness or anger—well, you'd better reach for that emotional dimmer switch and dial it way down low.

Two more problems now arise. (As I said, it's a slippery slope.) First, if you dial back this metaphorical dimmer in an attempt to mask or submerge your "negative" emotions, you're inevitably going to throttle your access to joy at the same time. Instead of becoming the Master of Your Emotions, you become the Master of No Emotions—at least, on the surface.

The second problem has shown up in earlier chapters. There is no such thing as "I am one person at work and another person at home." This is another self-limiting belief—in fact, one of the most insidious and damaging in our contemporary Western culture. What you shut down at work, you also shut down at home. I've heard some version of the following time and time again in my interviews with my clients' family members: "Dad is silent at dinner. His body is present, but his mind is somewhere else. Mom is putting on a brave face, but we know that she is very concerned about something that happened at work."

Again, there is no such thing as a separation of our personal and professional lives—and the attempt to separate them only damages both of them. And drains our energy far more than you realize.

## FIXING IT

So what is to be done?

The first thing to understand is that identifying and updating our belief systems takes a lot of curiosity. Why? Because for the most part, we don't even remember those deals that we cut so long ago and that rule our lives today. They tend to reside deep down in our subconscious minds.

But here's where the investments that you've made on previous levels begin to work in your favor. For example, your explorations of the emotional realm—on your path to self-love—give you the reserves of confidence and courage that you need to tackle the tough job of updating your belief system.

Keep in mind that your belief system is not your enemy; it's a misguided friend who doesn't know any better. It's been pieced together (by you) over the years to make you feel safe. Tackling your belief system is not like venturing into a cave to slay a dragon; it's more like having a very tough conversation with a difficult relative who's hiding behind a closed door.

And this brings up a key tactic for making the work that we need to do at Level 3 less daunting. For most of us, as illustrated by Helen's story and to some extent my own story, a huge obstacle to succeeding at this level is our blind loyalty to our parents and other loved ones. The very notion of questioning our belief system sometimes feels like a betrayal of their memory. If this is true in your case, and you carry these invisible loyalties, ask yourself, *What was my parents' most important goal when they instilled their belief system in me?* The two responses I hear most to this question are, "They wanted to protect me," and "They wanted to help me to be successful and happy."

And I'm sure that's true, in most cases. Well, what if some of these beliefs are outdated and no longer serve their original intention? What if they no longer protect you but now limit you and your happiness? What do you think your parents would do if they knew that some of the things they passed on to you are now adversely affecting you? Would they instantly give you permission to adapt or eliminate them? Of course they would. So changing your belief system is not a betrayal; it actually honors their memory.

## CHANGING YOUR MIND

Here's a good problem to have: when you go through a tough transition like Helen and come out the other side with your flags flying high—with new energy, purpose, and creativity— you may start to share the concern that sneaks up on many of my clients: *How can I make sure that this wonderful feeling of clarity and peace sticks? How can I make sure I don't lose it?*

To this question, I always reply, "First of all—enjoy the moment! And second, take comfort from the fact that your ability to access it today strongly suggests that it will be there for you tomorrow."

And after a little celebratory time has gone by, I drop the other shoe: But remember that there is no mastery without practice, practice, practice. It's a lifelong discipline.

How do you avoid having the muscle memory that comes along with a strict belief system or walls going back up from your protective systems? How can you change your mind—literally—and continue to grow your love of self (Level 2) and clarity of thought (Level 3)? Again, there are many answers. Remember the notion of intention, introduced in previous chapters? I find meditation with intention to be one of the most helpful resources for enabling a sustainable behavior change. Unfortunately, though, for most people, meditation doesn't provide enough of an immediate sense of reward or benefit, which is why many who have started doing it—including myself—have gotten frustrated with it and dropped it in favor of a faster, easier path.

What persuaded me to give it one more try, and ultimately got me hooked on it, was a book by Michael Pollan titled *How to Change Your Mind*.[2] Let me emphasize that I don't endorse Pollan's exploration of psychedelics as a way to change your mind, at least as I use the phrase.[3] But I do find his way of sharing his research and his wisdom about the brain—and the emotions grounded within it—fascinating. In a nutshell, neuroscientists have discovered the existence of an "orchestrator" in our minds, which they dubbed the Default Mode Network, or DMN. At one extreme, the DMN becomes too rigid—to the point that it takes full control of our mind, a condition that is associated with certain kinds of psychological disorders like OCD, schizophrenia, eating disorders, and so on. Conversely, when people are under the influence of psychedelics, the DMN effectively "goes to sleep"—and as a result, their brains go into a state of relative entropy.[4] Somewhat surprisingly, many psychedelic travelers come back from their trips with an enhanced ability to connect to loving feelings.

You can see where this is going. It appears that the DMN may be a formidable obstacle in our pursuit of sustainable behavior shifts. This was confirmed, indirectly, when researchers tried measuring the influence of the DMN in infants, and . . . couldn't even detect it! In other words, at that time in our lives when we are in a natural state of complete entropy, and our minds are more or less empty of thoughts, the DMN "thought policeman" is nowhere to be found.

My interpretation, connecting these dots: we are born with our minds empty and our hearts full of love. Perhaps this is the state of bliss that many of us try to get back to in so many wildly different ways.

One more data point that bears on what all this might have to do with meditation. In another stroke of methodological genius, our neuroscientists next decided to measure the DMN in expert meditators. They found that the DMN responds to meditation much as it does to psychedelics: it more or less goes to sleep. And with the right intention, practiced consistently, meditation appears to allow for sustainable behavior shifts to happen.

For our purposes, this is very good news indeed. As Richard Bandler, the cofounder of the field of neurolinguistic programming, remarked, "It's never too late to have a happy childhood."[5]

Of course, there are many different approaches to meditation. Poke around and find the one that feels right for you. Practice it at a time of the day that you can do it without feeling rushed. The most common first question I get: For how long? There's no one right answer, but I'd say, start small—five minutes max—and think of yourself as warming up to a bigger commitment. Make that bigger commitment as soon as you start experiencing some benefits from your discipline: that is, when you start feeling calmer, happier, more confident, less harsh on yourself, more loving to others, and so on. You'll want to make sure that these benefits keep increasing with your commitment—otherwise, you won't stick with it.

And no matter where you are on that path of commitment, keep in mind two essential ingredients. First, as I emphasized at Level 1, *be mindful of your breathing.* Second, *be intentional.* I've talked about this before. You are working toward an ever-increasing clarity of thought; with it comes additional acceptance of self. As acceptance grows, immense amounts of human energy will be released—benefiting both you and others around you.

What will it mean to your energy flow if you are feeling more pleasure, a felt sense through a physically healthy and strong body (Level 1), if you are emotionally centered in your relationship with yourself, and therefore more self-confident (Level 2), and if you are thinking clearly (rationally and intuitively), based on an updated belief system that exists to serve you, rather than the opposite (Level 3)? You will be in the zone. Your energy flow will increase dramatically, and you will make strides toward becoming a more humane leader.

## YOUR HOMEWORK FOR LEVEL 3

Within this chapter, my focus has been on the kinds of thoughts (beliefs) that may keep you from moving forward.

A key question to ask yourself at Level 3:
Can I be open, curious, and nonjudgmental about what I'm learning about myself and my belief system?

## SOME INTENTIONS TO SET FOR YOURSELF AT LEVEL 3

### Set the intention to update your belief system.

- What are my beliefs? What defines me? Who do I believe I am? Who do I believe I am not?
- Create a list in response to each question. Consciously engage your curiosity and creativity. When you're finished, study those lists for any changes that seem to be needed. Now look across the lists. Are there new and interesting ways to connect the dots? After you've made any necessary adjustments, bear down on your most recent version of that first list: *core beliefs*. Put the entries on that list through the following question, as a kind of filter: *Which beliefs make me feel safe?* Look at the top five and identify the beliefs that you would feel most uncomfortable about changing or even introducing into them some degrees of flexibility. Some of these beliefs may be rooted in your unconscious, so you may find it helpful to ask your family and friends to join in on these explorations. You are likely to be surprised about what you find together.
- Most likely, some of these beliefs will have to be retired. Others will need to be modified and updated. A precious few are candidates for the strongest possible embrace by you—an embrace that your ever-increasing clarity of thought will significantly amplify.
- Separate the beliefs that serve you from the ones that need an update.
- Looking at this latter group: If you could update these beliefs so that they could serve you better, how would you like them to be reworded?
- Once you've made the updates, read each belief out loud, one by one, and become curious about how you

feel about updating each of them. If the prospect of doing so makes you uncomfortable or anxious, ask yourself, *Why do I feel this way?* Remember Helen's story: sometimes we retain invisible loyalties to those people who passed their belief systems on to us.

## Set the intention to honor the original intention of your belief system.

- What were your caretakers' intentions when they passed their belief systems on to you? What were they hoping that those beliefs would help you achieve in life? If your answer to that question was happiness, success, or both, *be grateful,* and take the time needed to connect with this original intention from your caretakers.

- Now you can move forward with updating the beliefs that no longer serve you, knowing that you have honored your caretaker's original intention. As you connect to this original intention, read out loud the updates to the beliefs that you selected. How do you feel now? Do you feel at least somewhat more comfortable with the prospect of these updates? If so, good! You are on your way to living a life with more clarity of thought. Conversely, if your discomfort persists, find an ally who can help you explore why.

- Assuming that you feel more at ease with your updated beliefs, it's time to engage the power of meditation. This can be a relatively simple exercise. Start by visualizing how these updated beliefs will impact your life. (It may help to close your eyes.) Stay with the feeling that comes to you.

- Center your mind through silence and your body through breathing—inhaling through your nose and exhaling through your mouth in a relaxed, harmonious way. If you get distracted, take a deeper breath through your nose and be conscious of the air going through your lungs. This sensation will get you back into your body, back to silence, and thus, back to center.

- Do this meditation with intention for five minutes every day, at a time when your mind is as clear as possible. Keep this up until you feel that the updates to your belief system are now a part of you. Remember: the intention is to relax the Default Mode Network and enable more mental flexibility. Practice, practice, practice!

## THE TAKEAWAYS

❖ The third level within the human energy field focuses on clarity of thought. Your creative energy will encounter less friction and will have fewer distracting thoughts to deal with.

❖ Managing your energy at Level 3 enables a harmonious and complementary blend of rationality and intuition.

❖ To manage our energy at the third level of the human energy field, we need to update our belief system.

❖ The belief system is our internal rule book, which combines inherited beliefs and our own created beliefs. The first kind we accept at a time when our ability to discern is either nonexistent or severely limited. The second type we create for ourselves.

❖ Our belief system is also a protective mechanism, intended to keep us on the lookout and thereby buffer us from the hard knocks of our lives. When outdated, it can be self-limiting.

❖ Outdated belief systems can affect your ability to connect with your emotions (numbing them), or can encourage you to compartmentalize them (for example, "showing emotions at work is weak, while it is expected at home").

❖ Updating your belief system can create greater access to your intuition, amplifying your clarity of thought.

❖ Updating your belief system requires curiosity and courage. For the most part, we don't even remember when we included these beliefs in our rule book. One of the biggest obstacles to updating is the feeling of betrayal that comes from the blind loyalty we have to our caretakers.

❖ These beliefs were given to us with the best of intentions— to protect us. By updating our belief systems, we honor the original protective intention of our caretakers.

❖ Working toward an ever-increasing clarity of thought comes with additional acceptance of self. As acceptance grows, immense amounts of human energy will be released—benefiting both you and others around you.

❖ There is no free lunch. To change your mind, you need to adopt a discipline—meditation with intention is one way to do this—and then practice, practice, practice.

## Chapter 7

# Loving Interactions with Family and Friends (Level 4)

What happens when the children become givers and the parents become takers?

This happens far more often than we'd like to admit. Consider, for example, a family system within which the children take emotional care of the parents. Yes, the parents are in a sense lucky to have this kind of "expert" care—but at the same time, all kinds of dysfunctions can result.

Not so long ago, I had a client who grew up believing that she had to be a "perfect child." Why? Because her older sister was a mess, for most of her childhood, and her parents could barely cope with her. And given that her sister was creating so many waves, she felt that she shouldn't create *any*.

Somehow, she battled her way through into adulthood. When I met her for the first time, she was a highly successful executive. She was also taking care of her sister and their parents, both emotionally and financially, at the same time that she was raising her own family. She was truly besieged by all of these complex family dynamics; no surprise, then, when she told me that she felt that she had "no life."

We got to work. Through a focus on the Family Constellation model—introduced in earlier chapters and described more fully below—she came to realize that she had entanglements of both *order* and *balance*. In other words, she was both playing the wrong role, in terms of birth order, and was accepting responsibilities far beyond the fair demands of her role. Once she consciously assumed her place as Child Number Two (not Number One) and as sister (not parent) of her sister, her relationship with all her family members started improving. Interestingly, she used similar words to Emile's, as described in chapter 5: she told me it was like *a great weight was being lifted from her shoulders.*

She couldn't believe how much energy she derived from this. She's now even more successful at work, and she's leading a far, far happier and fuller life.

This level in the human energy field is associated with the *heart*, emotionally speaking. It involves giving and receiving love, in the specific context of the family, friends, and others in your inner circle. You'll recall that in the introduction I talked about the seven levels of energy within our human energy field, which I'm asking you to work on as part of your unique journey toward mastering your energy. Again, the first four levels are physical energy (Level 1), emotional energy (Levels 2 and 4), and mental energy (Level 3). This is the last of those four levels. By the end of this chapter, you'll have gone a long way down the road to energy mastery—and by extension, you'll be well on your way to becoming a humane leader.

Levels 5 through 7 focus on exploring and integrating spiritual energy: a challenge that you may or may not choose to take on. If you do, your work on this level—as well as Levels 1 through 3—will serve as an invaluable foundation.

Let me put that in stronger language: you need to work hard on these four levels before you can move on to greater challenges in your energy-mastery discipline.

Let's assume that you bring to this Level 4 challenge the tools that you mastered in our previous levels, especially your emotional acceptance of self and your clarity of thought—both of which have a profound impact on the quality of your interactions with your family and friends. In large part, your work on this level involves creating the space and making the time to be truly present with those people you love and bringing your loving presence to bear on those interactions. I'm avoiding the phrase *quality time*—which to me sounds too much like some precious ingredient, like saffron,[1] that's being measured and doled out. But "spending time engaged in high-quality interactions" is really what I'm talking about. So, instead, let's call it *intentional time*.

I've already touched on the importance of intentionality (chapter 4). Intentional time carries that idea forward. It requires you to bring your powers of clear thinking to bear on organizing and contributing to what is almost always a complex social structure—a family, a small community, or whatever. Maybe "clear thinking" and "social structure" sound like a mismatch, in the same way that calculation and spontaneity would not seem to fit together. But think about it. Most of us have a friend who is the glue that holds our circle of friends together. If they're lucky, families have one or two people in each generation who play the same role and take that role very seriously. They are not just playing at it; they're *working* at it. They're putting real thought and love into how they will strengthen bonds within the group.

Why are these important investments? In part because variety is, indeed, the spice of life. We need to give and receive love in many different kinds of relationships. We need to make time to be with friends and family, and remind ourselves as often as necessary that we are there with them to *love* them and to receive love from them. This applies even to the ubiquitous Uncle Lou—almost every family has one—who's on the wrong side of every political question that comes up. Getting the most out of Uncle Lou, as unlikely as that sounds, requires clear thinking and strong social structures to integrate him rather than ignore him.

You can and should contribute to that effort.

## IN THE WORKPLACE

How does this come to bear on the workplace and on the leader you want to become? Simple: people who are in trouble at home invariably bring those troubles to the workplace.

Let me underscore that: *invariably*. Most leaders I work with kid themselves on this score. They think they leave their troubles at home, but they don't. That ongoing struggle with your rebellious kid comes into the office and sits down in your chair with you, every day. Or phrased conversely and positively, those loving relationships that you've invested in away from work also come to work with you. They give you wonderful energy. They further clarify your thinking (Level 3)— by helping to sort out what's important and what isn't—which makes you more effective in your leadership role. When you're good with your loved ones, you're free to be at your best.

Of course, nobody's *always* at their best. The goal is to be conscious of where you are, *right now*, and work within that framework. Did you have a fight with your spouse this morning? Is a family member sick? Maybe you should put a little more time into caring for those at home, which might mean coming in to work an hour or two later than normal or leaving work earlier than normal. Again, this is the kind of *freedom of choice* that we're working toward, which frees up energy and incidentally frees up time. Maybe you should move one or two of today's scheduled meetings to another day, especially if you need to make a tough decision and your mind and heart will be more at home than at work. Or, if you absolutely *have* to attend one or more of those meetings, maybe this should be the day when you choose not to say very much.

This is the flip side of the challenge I've talked about in previous chapters: pretending that we can turn off our emotions at work and not damage our other human relationships. That can't happen. We're not robots. We're humans, bless us! And pretending that we're robots doesn't make us into robots. It just prevents us from tapping into and managing our human energy.

Just as on Level 2, some of the things that hold us back from releasing loving energy on Level 4 are ingrained within our *unconscious*. Breaking through this can be a complex challenge and is likely to require support from someone who is experienced in this work. It's a significant part of my interactions with many of my clients. By helping my clients achieve higher levels of self-awareness—that is, moving unconscious dynamics into the conscious realm and thereby resolving unconscious emotional entanglements in their relationships with their family and friends—I help those clients expand their freedom of choice.

There are many ways to get there. I find that one of the most effective approaches is the Family Constellation methodology created by German-born psychotherapist Bert Hellinger. En route to his ordination as a priest in the early 1950s, Hellinger was sent to South Africa, where he was assigned to serve as a missionary to the Zulus. Hellinger did indeed spend a decade and a half serving as a parish priest and running parochial schools; ultimately, though, his participation in a series of interracial trainings in group dynamics laid the groundwork for him to leave the priesthood and get certified as a psychotherapist in Germany.

In subsequent decades, he traveled extensively in search of ways to connect what he came to call the "collective unconsciousness." Family Constellation emerged as a part of this effort. Simply stated, Family Constellation brings order to the system, allowing the energy that is stuck between the family members to flow. This builds on some of the ideas I explained in the previous chapter. As the Hellinger organization explains it,

> Frequently, it is beliefs that we have inherited from our parents that keep us imprisoned. In the past, these were created in the subconscious and are now in our way. This prevents changes in behavior. In the Original Hellinger Family Constellations, our hidden beliefs come to light, can be questioned, released and overwritten.[2]

Hellinger preferred not to describe Family Constellation–related work as a form of therapy, and he resisted efforts to create a fixed theory or discipline around it. Nevertheless, its powerful principles have made it a useful tool in a wide variety of organizational contexts.

What are those principles? I can point to three.

## Bonding and Belonging

Every one of us has the right to belong to the family into which we were born. We are born into a family that goes back generations, and a child will do anything for the love of a parent. When the energy within the family system is clear and love flows, belonging and connections are a source of great strength. But when there is an interruption in the flow of energy—described by Bert Hellinger as an "entanglement"— the family system and the individuals within that system may be weakened. When an entanglement arises, your ability to get full access to the energy and strength that should flow at Level 4 may be unnecessarily constrained.

I've already presented several entanglement scenarios, including being born into a family system where your need to belong is not properly received. When this happens, we blame ourselves rather than our caregivers. We don't feel safe blaming our caregivers, and above all we want to feel safe. So we decide (incorrectly) that our current selves are "unlovable," and we therefore set out to create a new, more lovable self. We would rather think that we are not lovable than blame our caretakers or parents. As you can see, the unconsciousness at Level 4 is very much connected to the unconsciousness at Level 2 (self-love). Working on and healing the entanglements of Level 4 energy has a direct benefit to healing Level 2 energy, and vice versa.

Let's look back to earlier chapters and bring forward Emile Dorantz's story. You'll recall that he was wrestling with a Love of Self gap. I helped Emile address that gap by adopting the Family Constellation methodology. At first, he was more than a little skeptical about plunging into this kind of work. "Ricardo," he said, "I am only doing this because I fully trust you!"

With that qualified endorsement ringing in my ears, I made sure that I had the allies I needed to make this undertaking succeed. Again, it's important for coaches to understand where their limits lie. In that spirit, I invited Ester Martinez to join me in coaching Emile.[3] Ester worked with Bert Hellinger himself for close to twenty years, and she is one of my most cherished teachers; in fact, most of what I am sharing in this chapter grows out of my close client work with her.

So back to Emile: it was through the Family Constellation that Ester facilitated and that I participated in—playing the role of Emile's dad—that Emile arrived at some significant truths. He discovered that his fear of rejection dated back to when he was a young boy and his father left home, abandoning his family. Emile felt that abandonment acutely, deciding that he was not lovable. For Emile, it obviously was a deeply emotional experience to realize that there was still a young version of himself that was very much on the scene—an Emile who still needed to be seen, loved, and touched by his dad.

Getting in touch with this younger version of himself allowed Emile to feel *compassion* for this inner child and to begin to integrate his younger self into the adult Emile. At the same time, Emile discovered that he was able to forgive his dad, realizing that his father was a confused man who certainly didn't intend to wreak emotional havoc by persuading a little boy that he was abandoned for being unlovable.

Honestly, I get emotional just recalling this episode. Emile was courageous to go through this work. You can imagine that, at the end of our session, he was emotionally exhausted. And yet, as he told me later, he felt that he had been repaid many times over for that emotional investment.

## Order

Everyone belongs in a family system, including those individuals who for whatever reason are actively excluded. By extension, everyone has their own place in the order of the system. After Mom and Dad, the first child comes first, the second comes second, and so on.

Perhaps this sounds self-evident. But consider what happens when someone is cut out of that order—for example, the "black sheep" of the family. The whole system and everyone in the system is adversely affected by those who remain "unseen," whether lost or excluded. The complex parable of the Prodigal Son derives its power, in part, from our discomfort with the "disloyal" son who abuses his father's grace and leaves home—but also from our discomfort with the behavior of the other son, who doesn't want to welcome his brother back into the fold. Families have an *order*—an innate structure, with inherent expectations of those within it—and that order needs to be understood and respected.

## Balance in Relationships

This kind of balance is built over time, through exchanges of giving and taking. Again, at the risk of stating the obvious, for relationships to work, there has to be a give and take of love and respect. Between family members and friends—and, I'd argue, among colleagues at work—the balance is upset when there is too much of one and too little of the other. There's only one exception, and it's an obvious one: in the parent-child relationship, parents give and children take.

I first witnessed the benefits of the Family Constellation experience a little less than a decade ago. I recall being blown away by how effective Family Constellation was in contributing to behavioral breakthroughs on the part of the participant who volunteered to be the direct beneficiary of the work—at the center of the constellation, in other words—and also in delivering powerful benefits to those who participated either directly in the constellation or indirectly on the sidelines.

Since then, I've been part of Family Constellations for more than fifty of my clients. Without exception, these experiences—and the powerful principles that directed and propelled them—created an enhanced sense of family bonding, balance, and order. I should also say that I've used a tailored version of Family Constellation to untangle events in my own inner-family circle, where it again proved extraordinarily valuable in the way that we bond and love each other within my own family system.

So I've seen it firsthand, and can offer the following summary with great confidence. If you maintain your good health with the intention to have a felt sense in your body and, with it, feel more pleasure (Level 1), if your self-acceptance is centered (Level 2), if you soften your belief system to cultivate clarity of thought (Level 3), and you give and receive love from loving relationships with your family and friends

(Level 4), you will be well on your way toward having more freedom of choice in your life, you will be mastering your energy rather than managing your time, and while doing so, you'll make good progress toward becoming a humane leader. You will be newly able to bring your informed intuition to bear on your decision-making. You will be fueled by new reserves of energy. And finally, the creative powers that have helped distinguish you up to this point will be broadened and deepened.

That's not a bad stopping point, right? But I invite you to consider going on—either now, or sometime in your future—through the gateway described in chapters 8 and 9.

## WATCH OUT FOR BOOMERANGS!

One "watch-out" before we move forward to the next chapter and start to dip our toes in human spiritual energy: beware of the Boomerang Effect!

Doing good work on the first four levels of energy within the human energy field releases immense amounts of creative energy. You've taken off your personal and professional shield. You've embraced your physicality (Level 1), you are well into the process of love of self (Level 2), you are blessed with greater clarity of thought (Level 3), and you've gotten better at being at peace and more loving with your closest relationships (Level 4). As a result, you are at your best, or at least better than you were before you started your journey: physically, emotionally, and mentally. You are far more closely connected to your creative power.

Sounds great, right? So why the "watch-out"?

I'll invoke another metaphor, this time from the world of physics. Newton tells us that when one object exerts a force on another, the second object exerts an equal but opposite force on the first. Human energy reflects this same pattern. This is what I call the Boomerang Effect. Let's assume that you have become so connected to the energy inside you, and so *present*, that you unleash an enormous creative power. You are in the flow—in the zone—and your desire manifests, which is where you want to be and experience.

But this means that you are affecting other people's lives, and those people will certainly react to your new ways of doing and being. Those reactions will not always be positive. Sometimes people will make new and unwelcome demands on you. Other times, they may just push back because they don't like the changes that you've effected. And assuming that you've let down your shields by dialing back your fear system and belief system—as discussed in chapters 2 and 6—you are wide open to new inputs, both good and bad. Well, those bad (and sometimes even hostile) inputs can cause you pain again—the same pain that you've tried to avoid having, and the reason why you were unconsciously protecting yourself and were holding back in the first place! And if you're not aware and careful, your own "muscle memory" may feel compelled to raise that same old shield and put it back on again.

And that's serious. Once having lived through this kind of setback, you may not choose to go through the pain ever again. You may just decide to leave the old version of the shield on permanently.

Well, *don't* fall into this trap! Be aware of the Boomerang Effect, and don't flinch. Rather than interpreting these bumps in the road as personal attacks that have to be fended off, you should try to take them on board as learning opportunities. When you succeed at this—which probably won't be easy—it will enhance your confidence and motivation to venture forth and continue investing in your energy management, and the next time you experience the Boomerang Effect, it will be far less likely to confuse and hurt you.

I recently discussed the Boomerang Effect with Sarah, a potential CEO successor at a Fortune 100 company. In Sarah's case, her protective mechanisms were mostly rooted in the belief that achieving greater responsibilities necessarily came with sacrifice. As a result, her sense of duty was super high. She was always *on*, and her ability to set boundaries—especially for leaders within her organization—was quite limited. She maintained an open-door policy, which complicated her life a great deal. She understood these dynamics all too well—so, despite being the most eligible candidate to fill the soon-to-be-vacant CEO position, she didn't want to be considered for the role. She made sure that the outgoing CEO, the nominating committee of the board, and that committee's chair were aware of this.

Nobody was happy with this state of affairs—even Sarah, despite what she was thinking and saying. And thanks to the work that we did through unlocking her energy in Levels 1 through 4, Sarah came to the realization that if she worked on revising her belief system, and came to understand that it didn't have to be a sacrifice for her to become the next CEO, she could actually impose boundaries and take care of herself. In fact, she might actually be able to *enjoy* it! Where before she saw a golden cage, she now saw possibilities. When the brass ring finally came around in a formal way—the CEO position—she grabbed it.

And this, unfortunately, brings us to the Boomerang Effect. Sarah's increased self-confidence, combined with her new authority, led her to initiate big changes across the company. Many members of her team and peers felt the impact of her bold moves, some of which were well received but others of which sparked controversy. Both her admirers and detractors—more than a hundred people, by her informal count—sent word that they wanted to meet with her one-on-one and discuss the changes. If she had been guided by her previous belief system (*doing this job comes with a sacrifice!*), and if we hadn't already talked about the Boomerang Effect, Sarah might have felt compelled to open up space in her calendar for individual discussions with all (or at least most) of these people.

But that's not what happened. Instead, Sarah prioritized some calls, clustered many more of them into structured group sessions, and gently (but firmly) opted out of the rest. By all accounts, she approached these individual and group conversations with compassion and managed to shift her energy and theirs into a space of perceived opportunity, allowing her to still have time to do the things that gave her energy both personally and professionally.

## YOUR HOMEWORK FOR LEVEL 4

The analyses and prescriptions in this chapter all relate to *emotions that may get in your way.*

A key question to ask yourself at Level 4:
Can I be open, curious, and nonjudgmental about what I'm learning about myself and my emotional exchange with loved ones?

## SOME INTENTIONS TO SET FOR YOURSELF AT LEVEL 4

**Set the intention to connect your sense of belonging (Level 4) to your love of self (Level 2).**

- On a 1 to 10 scale, rate your sense of belonging within your family system of origin (your parents and siblings), with 1 being "I feel rejected" and 10 being "I belong." Remember: in this and other exercises, *speak truth.*

- Become curious about the rating you gave yourself. Why am I not a 10 out of 10? What past experiences do I recall that make me feel a gap in my sense of belonging with my family of origin?
- Use your journal to take note of these experiences, which often date back to an early part of your life.
- Cross-reference your Level 4 and Level 2 homework. Be curious about what you find when connecting these dots. Could these Level 4 stories from my past relate to the root cause of my Love of Self gap?
- The above question may be very helpful in case you get stuck—or you're not sure where you've really landed—in your search to find the root cause of your Love of Self gap.
- If you stay stuck, this may be all the more reason to find an ally to help you in your quest to center your emotional energy (Level 2 and Level 4)—and if you do, your ally will now have more information.

**Set the intention to be in your
rightful place in your family and at work.**

- Am I in my rightful place within my family system, and do I behave accordingly? If I am sibling number three out of three, for example, do I play that role—or do I try to be the older brother, or even the dad or mom?
- Am I in my rightful place at work, and do I behave accordingly? Or do I take more or greater responsibilities than my role requires?
- Compare your answers to the questions above and be curious. What surprises you? Do you behave differently at home and at work or the same? Most likely, your behavior patterns at home duplicate the ones you

exhibit at work. Nonparents who behave at home like parents to survive and thrive are likely to bring that parental energy at work, which makes it very difficult for them to set boundaries. Does this resonate with you? If so, then you are probably very good at taking care of people but not so good at taking care of yourself.

- Breaking these patterns of system disorder can release immense energy. Conversely, *not* doing so will continue to give energy away—and increase the likelihood that you'll pass on these behavioral patterns to your own children.
- Engage in meditation with intention.

Bringing these unconscious behaviors to the level of consciousness is a way to start to break these patterns, and meditation can help.

Visualize how this new level of awareness will affect your life, and stay with the feeling that comes to you. Once again, it may help to close your eyes. Contemplate how being in your place and behaving accordingly will impact your life, and begin your meditation.

The technique here is the same as described in previous chapters: Center your mind through silence and your body through breathing. Inhale through your nose and exhale through your mouth in a relaxed, harmonious way. If you get distracted, take a deeper breath through your nose and be conscious of the air going through your lungs. This sensation will get you back into your body, back to silence, and thus, back to center.

Do the meditation with intention for five minutes, each day, at a time when your mind is as clear as possible. Do it until you feel that being in your place feels natural to you.

Practice, practice, practice!

### Set the intention to bring balance—
### giving and taking—to your relationships.

- I purposefully left this part of the homework to the end. Until you have a healthy sense of belonging and ordering in your family system, your ability to create a healthy balance in giving and taking in your relationships will be limited. But you don't have to wait to feel a *complete* sense of belonging and order before starting on this intention. Once you are on your way to getting that sense, ask yourself the following questions:

> Do my relationships at home give me energy or take energy away from me?
>
> Do my relationships at work give me energy or take energy away from me?
>
> Be curious about these two answers. Are there common patterns?
>
> What is holding me back from bringing a healthier balance into my relationships? Connect the dots. What did I discover when bringing balance to my sense of belonging and when taking my rightful place within my family system?
>
> Take advantage of this opportunity to explore the root cause that affected your feeling of belonging.

## THE TAKEAWAYS

❖ This level in the human energy field involves giving and receiving love in the specific context of the family, friends, and others inside your inner circle.

❖ This is the last level to work on to master your physical, emotional, and mental energy, before you decide to work and integrate spiritual energy in your path to becoming a humane leader.

❖ Your work on this level involves creating the space and making the time to be truly present with those people you love and bringing your loving presence to bear on those interactions.

❖ People who are in trouble at home invariably bring those troubles to the workplace. They think they leave their troubles at home, but they don't. Pretending that we can turn off our emotions at work doesn't work; in fact, it prevents us from tapping into and managing our human energy.

❖ Some of the things that hold us back to release loving energy at Level 4 are ingrained within our unconscious and are likely to require support from someone who is experienced in this type of personal work. Find an ally!

❖ There are many ways to get there. I find that one of the most effective approaches is the Family Constellation methodology created by German-born psychotherapist Bert Hellinger.

❖ If you maintain your work and practice from Levels 1 through 4, you will be well on your way toward having more freedom of choice—managing your energy rather than your time—and becoming a humane leader.

## Chapter 8

# The Gateway—Connecting Physical and Spiritual Energy

For two reasons, the Statue of Liberty in New York's harbor serves as a useful metaphor for opening this brief chapter.

**Reason #1:** This chapter is about a gateway, and Lady Liberty serves as a figurative gateway to New York Harbor. Since its dedication in 1886, the statue has provided the first and most enduring impression of the United States of America for countless immigrants. Those people had made a conscious and courageous choice, and passing by that statue—going through that gateway—must have been an inspiring and anxiety-provoking moment for many.

**Reason #2:** A present-day visit to the statue involves a series of gateways—that is, openings along the path of your visit that you can choose either to go through or not go through. For example, you can simply tour the grounds of Liberty Island without entering the statue itself. Alternatively, if you secure a pedestal pass, you can access the monumental structure at the base of the statue. To get to the visitors' level at the top of the pedestal, you enter the statue and climb 215 stairs—or you can take the elevator if you want. Either way, once you get to the top of the pedestal you are rewarded with spectacular views of New York City, New Jersey, and the harbor, and you can visit the island's museum. If you stop your explorations there, in other words, you will have been amply rewarded.

But! There's an additional gateway and an additional option: going all the way up into the statue's crown. This requires climbing another 146 steps, and at this gateway, you find that there's no elevator. It's crowded quarters on that staircase, and in the summer months, hot and stuffy. Climbing from the base to the crown is the equivalent of twenty-seven flights of stairs—in other words, *hard work*. But I have done it, and I assure you that the view from the crown is well worth all of those 361 steps.[1]

I invoke the statue here because touring Liberty Island involves confronting gateways—portals—and making choices. On your journey to learning how to master your energy and becoming a humane leader, you similarly encounter gateways and make choices. Levels 1 through 4, described in the previous chapters, present a clearly defined set of challenges. If you work hard enough at overcoming those challenges, you will enjoy powerful benefits. As I've said before, you can decide to end your journey there—at the top of our metaphorical pedestal—and know that you've done great work already for you and for others.

Or you can continue to climb.

## FROM THE PHYSICAL TO THE SPIRITUAL

Level 4 is the point of demarcation between the physical energy—expressed in the first four levels of the human energy field—and the spiritual energy, described in the next three chapters.[2] Some readers may already be familiar with this boundary; others may not be. For you to get access to this gateway and pass through it successfully, you absolutely have to put in the work that's needed on the first four levels, always with the concept of *intentionality* in mind. (Again, see chapter 4.) Musicians have to play their scales, endlessly, before they can achieve proficiency. Athletes have to develop muscle memory. You have to plug away at Levels 1 through 4 before moving on, always remembering *why* you're plugging away.

Why all this talk about gateways and choices? Let me start to answer that question by quoting Eva Pierrakos, a Viennese-born mystic and healer whose work in the United States led to the creation of a movement focused on her teachings and writing: the International Pathwork Foundation.[3] Pierrakos wrote more than two hundred lectures, which today serve as the core of the foundation's work. In one of them, she writes about "the gateway" in a way that I find helpful and moving:

> Through the gateway of feeling your weakness lies your strength; through the gateway of feeling your pain lie your pleasure and joy; through the gateway of feeling your fear lie your security and safety; through the gateway of feeling your loneliness lies your capacity to have fulfillment, love and companionship; through the gateway of feeling your hate lies your capacity to love; through the gateway of feeling your hopelessness lies true and justified hope; through the gateway of accepting the lacks of your childhood lies your fulfillment now.[4]

It has taken me more than a few years to understand and feel how the gateway between physical and spiritual energy works—and its relevance for us, as humans, in our efforts to master our energy.

By way of introduction, my definition of "spirituality" is the journey whereby we earn back our ability to fully experience unconditional love—what others will refer to as our original bliss. Let me be very clear on this point: for me, spirituality is *not* religion or a particular religious belief that is shared and observed by a group. Instead, it's an individual practice. It focuses on achieving a greater sense of peace and meaning in one's life.

You've heard some of this in previous chapters, presented in slightly different language. When we came into this world, we arrived with our heart completely full (emotional energy) and our head completely empty (mental energy), with nothing impeding our energy flow. To me, that sounds like bliss: a state of complete happiness or joy. But as I've shared in previous chapters, as our lives unfolded, we inevitably experienced hurt or pain. To buffer ourselves against further trauma, we created protective balancing systems—fears and beliefs—and gradually shaped and strapped on our personality, which includes our shields, professional and personal.

All this shaping and strapping on came at a price. During the creation of our personality, we forgot who we were. We disconnected from our original state of bliss. Since then, wittingly or unwittingly, consciously or unconsciously, we've tried to get back to that blessed state. But think about that quest and why it's important. Frankly, when we were babies, we couldn't *do* anything with the powerful loving energy that suffused us; we could only live it. But as adults, gaining access to that loving energy gives us the power to do truly amazing things.

By doing self-discovery work at the first four levels of human energy, as described in the previous four chapters, you learn how to get access to the physical, emotional, and mental energy within yourself. You gain the ability to create wonderful things for yourself and others within your close circle of family and friends. By extension, these changes also come to bear on the workplace. The love that you create at home inevitably follows you to work—and that's a great thing indeed.

Even then, though, you may start to feel that something is still missing. You may be achieving great professional success and yet find yourself wondering if there is still more that you're capable of achieving.

The answer is almost certainly yes. First, there's more ground to be gained on the earlier levels—the levels of physical, mental, and emotional energy—but you can get there only by embracing a more explicit and *intentional* spiritual quest. Committing to doing it will give greater meaning to the work you've already done within the first four levels, and as you will see, the spiritual quest described in Levels 5 through 7 will have power and rewards of its own.

Whenever I broach the subject of spiritual energy with my clients, a standard two-step process tends to get initiated. First, the person I'm talking with expresses a kind of respectful skepticism: "Well, that's all well and good for someone like you to focus on, Ricardo; but I'm out here trying to keep things together in the real world." But then, almost immediately, I start to hear tons of *questions*. These aren't questions intended to challenge; instead, they come from a place of deep curiosity and sometimes deep longing. By and large, the person I'm talking with genuinely wants to know more.

Those are the kinds of questions I raise and attempt to answer in the next three chapters.

## WE ALL START AS BEGINNERS

Most of us are novices when it comes to exploring spiritual energy—and, in fact, we all *start* as novices on this particular road.

Meanwhile, most of my clients are successful in part because of their innate curiosity. So it's no surprise when they bring their curiosity to bear on this new topic—spirituality—I've introduced. Here, I may surprise you: at this point, I always recommend that my clients put their curiosity to the side, for the time being, and devote their energy to learning about—and perhaps diving into—the fifth, sixth, and seventh levels of human energy.

I suggest that you do the same. For the time being, think of spirituality as that exotic place where you've never gone because it has always struck you as maybe a tad *too* exotic . . . but at the same time, you've always thought of it as intriguing . . . and likely you've never actually *crossed it off* your bucket list . . .

But to tee up the chapters that follow, and to keep you at least curious *enough,* I offer this quote from mythologist Joseph Campbell:

> If you do follow your bliss, you put yourself on the kind of track that has been there all the while, waiting for you, and the life that you ought to be living is the one that you are living. . . . Follow your bliss and don't be afraid, and doors will open doors where you didn't know they were going to be.[5]

*Following your bliss*: a journey that Campbell said began within yourself. We will return to Campbell, and bliss, later in the book.

## Chapter 9

# Speaking and Following Your Truth (Level 5)

Before the COVID pandemic, a colleague and I facilitated a very complex CEO succession process.

One of the internal candidates—let's name her Gabi—was likely to be selected by the nominating committee, but in the middle of my conversations with Gabi, she started expressing significant doubts about accepting the opportunity if the board extended the formal invitation to her. As our sessions went by, she sharpened up her reasons for *not* taking the job if it was offered to her. "Why *should* I do it," she asked rhetorically, "if I'm already fulfilled by my current responsibilities and when taking this new challenge puts many things at risk, both personally and professionally? I don't need to do this!"

Trying to sound supportive rather than argumentative, I asked her, "Gabi, are you really fulfilled? When was the last time that you felt really happy?"

"Honestly?"

"Honestly."

"Okay." She thought about it for a moment. "Speaking truth, the last time I felt really happy was when I was in my early twenties. We were on a family vacation."

I noticed that she had half closed her eyes while sharing this memory. I immediately asked her to connect to this truth and answer the following question: Why are you hesitating to take this next opportunity that life is offering to you?

She looked away. "The truth is, I'm afraid that this new opportunity will take me further from finding my sense of joy in life. I'm already very successful, right? I don't believe that more success in this same vein is going to give me what I am longing for."

"Which is?"

"To feel more *alive* again."

Sometimes the biggest lies are the ones that we tell ourselves. For years Gabi had been telling herself, "I'm successful and fulfilled!" But her *truth* was, "I am successful and unfulfilled!" Summoning up the seemingly unrelated truth about when she was last happy opened up this door, as well, surprising her with her own answer: Her *real* issue was her longing to feel more alive again.

So I pressed forward. "What if this new opportunity gave that back to you? What if, under the right circumstances, it became a renewed source of energy for you? And what would those circumstances be?"

The conversation immediately shifted, as she allowed herself to start moving into a high-energy place. "Well," she replied, "if I dare to dream, I'd love to connect this role and its potential impact to *benefit society* . . ."

Off to the races! Once she envisioned a connection between this new position and her true purpose in life, she began to see opportunity, excitement, and *energy*, where before she only saw risk and downside. Long story short: she took the job when it was offered to her—more or less on her terms—and she has emerged as a very successful CEO. And she tells me that now that her energy is intentionally connected to her purpose—to her *truth*—she is also experiencing a more fulfilled life.

Level 5 captures the power of the spoken word in your creative process. As you work on this level, you are pursuing *clarity* in your life. You are sidestepping the corrosive power of lies and other distortions and, instead, are trying to articulate and embody the *truth*, as you understand it.

There are several ways to think and talk about truth. I've come to think of it in terms of *speaking and following your personal truth*. So this part of our journey starts with one of the biggest questions we can ask ourselves: *Why am I here?* What is my life task? What's my life's purpose?

It's certainly not a new question. Discovering why you are here is one of the most compelling and enduring of all human desires. But it is especially important in your *self*-discovery. Figuring out your true purpose points you toward your life's destination and helps you fend off the distractions and distortions that drain away your energy. Knowing why you are here enables you to separate the noise from the truth. It helps you identify distorted desires and push them away in favor of the desires that will bring you closer to your personal truth.

Even if you're one of those lucky few who knows why you are here, I encourage you to keep reading through to the end of the chapter. I think you'll benefit from thinking about your life task in new and different ways.

## AT HOME AND AT WORK

Let's begin on a trivial level. Think about how many times in the course of a day you say things that you know are not true. For example: think about those little white lies at home—mostly designed to paper over difficult situations and certainly not intended to mislead or do damage. And yet, don't you usually find yourself delivering them with a little dose of *irritation* behind them? That's because unconsciously, or even consciously, you don't *want* to be in the position of distorting the truth. We know in our bones that falsehoods have consequences. Yes, in many cases the truth would have had consequences too—that's why we duck the truth in favor of fibs—but coming up with the fib and then maintaining it over time distracts us. Keeping our false stories straight consumes energy.

Now think about the worst meetings at work. Those are the ones about which people fail to tell the truth when they're setting the meeting up, fail to tell the truth during the meeting, and fail to report truthfully on the meeting after it's over. Ugh.

*So what?* you might ask. This happens all the time, right? Not a big deal? But in fact, it *is* a big deal. A meeting like that not only wastes your time—that time you don't have enough of?—but it also drains away energy. On both a conscious and unconscious level, it's *demoralizing*. Picture a bucket with a small hole in the bottom. That's not water draining out the bottom of the bucket; that's the energy that you and other participants have poured into this meeting going to waste. Little lies make you anxious and make you inclined to fix things; structural lies (like meetings with holes in the bottoms of their metaphorical buckets) drain you.

Now let me go out on a limb and offer at least a partial answer to your Biggest Question: *You are here to speak, embody, and act upon the truth as you see it—all the time, anywhere.* You need to root out the baseless insecurities and distorted desires that encumber you—like hobbles on your feet—and step forward purposefully. What truth do you speak for, and how are you going to act upon it? Like Gabi, you stand for something good. How are you going to advance that cause?

Maybe you're already running through the list in your head of circumstances in which you can't act on your truth. Maybe (1) your boss is a legitimately difficult person to deal with, and (2) you won't stay employed if you tell him or her your whole truth, and (3) you need to stay employed. So, okay, there *are* moments where you won't be able to hold to 100 percent of your truth. It goes with the territory. But at least you've identified the problem, and that's *really important*. You've made a choice, and you're dealing with it. But now, if you're going to master your energy, you need to make your *next* choice.

Yes, easier said than done. But the longer you thwart yourself, the more energy you will waste. Meanwhile, as long as it doesn't violate your values or your principles, how about, "I disagree with you, boss. I wouldn't do it that way if I were you. But you're the boss, and of course I'll commit to trying to make your plan succeed." At least, in that case, you're talking truth from a place when you are emotionally grounded. The bucket isn't leaking. And your hunt for the next, truth-supporting job can begin when it begins.

## TAKING ACTION . . . IN TIME

You need to commit to speaking and following your truth. Failing to do so risks undoing some of the hard work you've already been engaged in. It will eat away at your self-confidence (Level 2), prevent you from thinking clearly (Level 3), spill into and negatively affect your loving relationships (Level 4), and may even make you sick (Level 1).

Let me rephrase all that in positive terms. The tools you've picked up in previous levels will now come to your aid. If you're feeling well, if you're confident with yourself, and if you feel supported by your loved ones, you will feel safe(er)—and it will be *far easier* to go to a place of truth and far easier to act based on your truth.

We are now entering the realm of the spiritual, which means that, increasingly, the disciplines you need are to be found inside yourself. People may not appreciate hearing your truth, especially if you've kept quiet about it for a long time (remember the Boomerang Effect I shared with you in chapter 7). This certainly isn't reason enough to tell something *other* than your truth because as we've already determined, dissembling is corrosive, undermining, and energy draining. But speaking difficult truths that have been left unsaid tends to create new kinds of exposure for you and may leave you vulnerable.

With that in mind, you may want to avoid contact with those people in your life who've established themselves as aggressive skeptics. Not forever, certainly; just for the time being. Pace yourself. Not everyone needs to hear your truth *right now*, and that includes the truth about you. Very often when we are closing out a client retreat, one of the key recommendations that we make is that our participants take a figurative moment to catch their breath. Through a week of deep introspection, they've arrived at what in many cases are life-changing breakthroughs. "Yes, you'll want to act on those discoveries," we say. "But you can take the time to create a little space between discovering your truth and sharing that truth with your loved ones and with the world."

And then act!

## ENGAGING DIVINE WILL

Not speaking and embodying your truth as best as you can—anytime, anywhere—hurts you. It diminishes your ability to tap into your human energy. Earlier, I asked you to think about your life's purpose. Now, think about how your life purpose intersects, and interacts, with your creativity.

When you are creating from a place where your life's purpose and your personal truth are not in alignment, you may well enjoy the kinds of achievement that the people around you consider to be "success," but there's a very good chance that *you will not feel completely fulfilled*. This was Gabi's problem. She felt that, deep within her, something was missing. Despite the success, there's a void.

As noted, to succeed at Level 5, you need to call upon all the new resources you've been developing at previous levels. And there's one more ingredient that you'll have to add to the mix. I'll call it "divine will"—and by that I mean an energy source that up until now you probably haven't tapped into. It's inside you and also outside you. In chapter 8, I focused on the notion of a gateway. Imagine a door that opens into a new dimension of candor and care—like a heavy old oak door at the entrance to a library or any other place where wisdom might reside. Your work on Level 5 starts to pry that door open. And as soon as it does, it starts to make it easier for you to succeed on Level 5 and beyond.

I speak from personal experience. To gain access to the world of spiritual energy, I had to trust and follow divine will, even when I didn't understand what it was about (that understanding came later). Let me share some of what I eventually pieced together.

The phrase *divine will* has been misused a great deal and is often misunderstood. One traditional way of thinking about divine will carries with it an implicit obligation to challenge authority. In other words, divine will is something that we must defy to be truly free—and fortunately or unfortunately, we're endowed with the free will that enables us to *choose* to challenge. So, from this perspective, we are caught in a divine-will dilemma. You'd better put up a fight—and you may get in hot water if you do!

In a second conventional way of thinking, divine will is something to fear. If we don't figure it out and follow it, we'll be punished. This, too, puts us in a bind, and it raises some interesting choices. For example, if we never bother to figure out what our divinity's will is, well, maybe we won't be punished so severely when we stray off the path. So let's not figure it out!

A third conventional and fundamentally negative way of looking at divine will is predestination. In this view, the universe and all its doings are all prewired, anyway. But if there's nothing we can do to change divine will, we're off the hook entirely, right? So let's really hope that we're among the Chosen!

Note that in all these conceptions of divine will, all of the power resides *outside of ourselves*. This effectively relieves us of responsibility for our own fate. Even in those worldviews that do assign us some individual responsibility by admonishing us to be "good"—as in, *behave yourself and you may get what you want*—"good" comes across as something that is simultaneously constraining and difficult to achieve. And note that even when divine will is seen as something that gives us the power to overcome resistance, both the obstacle and the solution to that obstacle are entirely outside ourselves. We are pawns and proxies in a bigger battle.

All these negative conceptions of divine will separate us not only from others but—more important—from ourselves. When we are separated from ourselves, we are separated from our spiritual energy. Accepting any of these beliefs sets us up to live our lives with our hands tied.

Here's another way to look at it:

- Divine will is within us as well as outside of us.
- The choices we make "of our own free will" have to conform with the divine will that is inside us, or they will cause dissonance and a loss of energy.

During another complex succession process, my client John was convinced that he wanted to accept the invitation from the board's nominating committee to become his company's next CEO. In fact, he was quite energized by the prospect. Well, by that point, I'd been coaching John for a couple of years, so we knew each other well, and for me, something was lacking coherence. So, the week before he was scheduled to present his case to the board to win their support for his promotion, I asked him the question that had been troubling me.

"John," I began. "As your adviser, I think I owe it to you to ask this question. Which part of you is driving the decision to accept—is it your ego or your heart?"

Not surprisingly, John was quite upset at that. "Ricardo—how could you even *ask* me that, this close to the moment of truth? Not fair!"

I didn't agree or disagree; I just asked him to please sleep on the question and reconvene the next day, to which he somewhat reluctantly agreed.

The next morning, John was in a much better place. He said that even though he had tossed and turned a good deal the night before, he had wound up grateful that I had posed my question to him. "I appreciate your courage and care, Ricardo," he said graciously. "You helped me realize that my decision was being driven by my ego rather than by my heart, and so my case to the board was mostly built around what I thought they wanted to hear, rather than what I'd like to do if I were honored with the opportunity to serve in that role. And as I think you already know, that's not fair either to them or to me."

Based on that insight, he started to articulate what his heart wanted to tell the board—including the candid statement that if he couldn't be picked based on speaking his truth, then the job wasn't meant for him. He didn't need much encouragement from me in thinking this through out loud. It was *his* truth, after all.

He made more or less the same declaration during his next meeting with the board. I'm happy to report that they were so inspired by the "real" John that he got the role with their unanimous support. They also pledged to do their best to help him be successful in delivering on his mandate.

Both Gabi and John knew something about themselves, but they could see it only with what I'd call their peripheral vision. I'm sure you've had that experience—of seeing something that's just out of your direct sight but is nevertheless *real* and *there*. Divine will, inside us and outside of us, is for me one of those things.

For example? When I began thinking about writing this book, I found that I was constantly fighting with myself. I seized upon every excuse not to start: I was too busy at work, my family couldn't spare me, I had no experience as an author, my colleagues might think I was getting too big for my britches, and so on, and so on. But deep within me, I knew that I owed it to the people who aspired to become humane leaders to sit down at the keyboard and *get on with it*. I knew that if I was really going to fulfill my life's purpose, this was an essential step to take.

As my "humble" example begins to illustrate, doing what we believe our divine will is telling us to do is not usually the *easiest* path. So it's a really good idea to reality-test your emerging plan ("writing a book"). In the following sections, I share some questions to help you determine if you are aligning yourself with your divine will.

## YOUR HOMEWORK FOR LEVEL 5

Within this chapter, my analyses and prescriptions focus on the power of the spoken word in your creative process.

A key question to ask yourself at Level 5:

Can I be open, curious, and nonjudgmental about what I'm learning holds me back from speaking my truth?

## SOME INTENTIONS TO SET FOR YOURSELF AT LEVEL 5

### Set the intention to speak truth anytime, anywhere.

Here, I'm happy to pass along the questions that Barbara Ann Brennan challenges you to ask yourself before you speak your truth:[1]

- If I connect with my truth, what is it that I need to say?
- What have I kept quiet about for a long period of time?
- Why haven't I expressed what I believe is true?

Write your answers to these questions in your journal. Write your way through all these questions fairly quickly—that is, without overthinking your responses—and put the result aside for a day or two. Then go back and work your way through the questions and your answers again. Is there still more about your truth that you should be telling?

### Set the intention to discover your life's purpose.

Many books, including some great books, have been written in an attempt to answer questions like: Why am I here? What is my life's purpose? What are the benefits that I'll gain by living a life with meaning?[2]

And even though good ideas abound in this realm, I want to provide clarity as to the "how" at Level 5. So, rather than giving you questions to solve for discovering your life's task, I'm going to give you a homework ritual that has been very helpful to leaders seeking to answer these Big Questions. It's important for you to understand that this ritual takes approximately three hours to do properly. Once you start, you can't take a break and start up again later. It also won't work if you pursue shortcuts. In other words, if you don't have the time or the mindset to go through it, it's better not to start it.

That said, this ritual is to be *enjoyed*. Wait for the right moment, and go for it!

The ritual is called Purpose Quest, and I first experienced it under the guidance of a wise friend named Sander Tideman.[3]

For your Purpose Quest assignment to work its magic, it needs to be conducted not at home but in nature. To prepare, you need to bring with you only a notebook, a pen, and your innate curiosity. The first step is to reflect on your key question—what breakthrough do you want to achieve? What does your heart long for? It could be as big as discovering your life's purpose. An ally can help you get this question clear. Formulate this in a concise, positively stated question and write it down. Then head off to the edge of some woods and find a stick of some sort. Now pick a random starting point, place the stick in front of you, and declare an intention. For example, for the purpose of this chapter, you might say, "As I step beyond this stick, I enter this forest with the intention of discovering my life's purpose." Be decorous about it. Get into the *ceremonial* aspects of it. (This is serious stuff.)

Now take a hike for twenty or thirty minutes, keeping an eye out for a spot up ahead of you that strikes you as beautiful. A spot that somehow calls to you. As you continue to walk toward that spot, become mindful of what your senses are taking in. Be aware of what you hear, smell, and see, and have a felt sense of the experience (Level 1), taking notes in your notebook on whatever comes into your head. It doesn't matter if it doesn't make sense; just write it down.

Once you reach the spot, get comfortable, because you are going to remain there for two hours. Some people find this easy, but a larger number find spending two hours by themselves in the forest an unsettling experience. Why? Because the only place to go is within yourself—and if you are not used to going there, it may be a difficult journey. In either case, *hang in there*. Just try to practice "natural awareness" by paying attention to the moment-to-moment experience, without thinking about it. As the time goes by, continue to log in all the reflections that come into your head (Level 3) and into your heart (Levels 2 and 4), no matter how crazy they may seem. Very likely, the longer you sit there, the more illogical your thoughts and emotions are likely to become. It is important to refrain from interpreting these experiences while you are on your spot in nature; just let them arise and flow, and return to natural moment-to-moment awareness all the time.

After the two hours are over, return in silence to the place where you started your Purpose Quest. Stop just short of the stick that you placed there several hours earlier, and—breaking your silence—offer thanks to nature for hosting you on your quest.

Now find a place where you can sit comfortably—preferably still in nature—and take a good read of your log. Let the words go deep, and stay with you. (This will help you remember what you felt and experienced when you ventured beyond the stick.) Once you've reconnected with those memories, the next step is to distill the essence of the ritual. Select ten words from your path before finding the spot, and another ten words from the scribbles you made while you were sitting in the spot you selected. Again, don't overthink it; just feel and favor the words that come to you naturally. You can complement this with creating images and put them into a drawing. Any artistic expression can be helpful, as it expresses your intuition rather than your logical thoughts. Once you have your twenty words, spend the next thirty minutes or so creating your version of a *haiku*[4]—a structured type of short Japanese poetry—focused on defining the purpose in your life. Try creating a couple of these, consciously trying to be bold and daring while you're doing so. (Again—this is important stuff, right? It's your life's purpose.) Once you've finished several, read them out loud, allowing yourself to feel the power of your words. Pick the one that moves you the most, and read it again out loud as if you were declaring its power to the world. Stay with that feeling for a few minutes, savoring the power of your words, the power of the truth within you. If you feel as moved as I did when I performed this ritual, you may want to declare the results openly to your family and friends, to your organization, and perhaps to society.

This sets the stage for creating a symbolic space: the last step of the Purpose Quest. First, find three rocks that include some kind of point, roughly like an arrow. Place them on the ground with one pointing north, another east, and the last one south, with something like six feet separating them and creating a square with one corner missing (the western corner). Now visualize the square as a circle, with the four corners being located on its perimeter. The "entrance" to this circle is from the west, where the rock is missing.

You're going to enter this circle—but before you do, walk around it three times in a clockwise direction. Then declare your haiku out loud, and ask for permission to enter the circle. You will feel that permission when it arrives (which it will). Once inside the circle, look to the north and visualize your closest loved ones. Then say something to the effect of, "I present to my loved ones my life's purpose," and again, declare your haiku out loud. Feel your words, and allow yourself to be moved.

Then turn to the east and do the same. This time, though, you will visualize society instead of your loved ones. Then turn to the south and repeat the process, this time visualizing your organization or team. Notice any differences in how you feel, based on the people to whom you are declaring the result of your Purpose Quest. Once you have finished your declarations, leave through the "door" of the west and bow toward the circle to show your respect and to declare the ritual ended.

I've performed this Purpose Quest ritual with clients who were longing to find their purpose as a source of direction and energy, and most of whom have found the experience liberating and enlightening. In fact, several of them have their haiku printed at their desk, and whenever they feel that their purpose is being challenged, they look at it as a source of centering and inspiration.

Is the Purpose Quest a silver bullet? No. It probably won't present you with the full, final discovery of your life's purpose. But is it worth trying? Yes! It's a terrific, nonmental way to jump-start your efforts to answer one of humanity's Biggest Questions: Why am I here?

Perhaps you're curious what I learned about my life's purpose, through the Purpose Quest and other techniques. It was both simple and infinitely complex, as I shared in the introduction: to help leaders with impact *connect to and manage their energy to become humane leaders.* To me, that has been extremely helpful.

### Set the intention to connect your life's purpose to divine will.

- On a scale of 1 to 10, with 1 being dissatisfied and 10 being fulfilled, rate how fulfilled you are. When was the last time you were really happy? Be curious and honest with yourself. When your life's purpose and your personal truth are not in alignment, despite how successful you are, there's a very good chance that *you will not feel completely fulfilled.* If you're not, this is a good thing to know!

- When you're making the most relevant decisions in your life, is it your ego making the choice, or are you connecting to your creative power (self)?
- Are your choices connected to the purpose of your life?
- Does your will turn you in the direction of your freedom?
- Does it empower you to fulfill your deepest longing?

When you discover your life's purpose, that purpose becomes your North Star. It serves as a shining destination that shields you from distorted desires along the path of your journey. Combined with divine will, it reinforces what is true to you. You are speaking your truth, as described in Level 2, which helps you close the self-love gap. You are achieving greater clarity of thought (Level 3) and generating more love for and from family and friends (Level 4).

As I've stressed earlier, all these energy levels exist in relation with one another. Each liberates the others. By integrating your spiritual energy with your physical, emotional, and mental energy, you tap into huge reservoirs of additional energy that awaits within you—and which can't be reached any other way.

## THE TAKEAWAYS

❖ Level 5 captures the power of the spoken word in your creative process. As you work on this level, you are pursuing *clarity* in your life, trying to articulate and embody the *truth*, as you understand it.

❖ Figuring out our true purpose points us toward our life's destination and helps us fend off the distractions that drain away our energy.

❖ Knowing why we are here enables us to separate the noise from the truth. It helps us identify distorted desires and push them away in favor of the desires that will bring us closer to our personal truth.

❖ *You are here to speak, embody, and act upon the truth as you see it—all the time, anywhere.*

❖ The tools you've picked up in previous levels will now come to your aid. If you're feeling well (Level 1), if you're confident with yourself (Level 2), if you feel supported by your loved ones (Level 4), it's *far easier* to go to a place of truth and it's far easier to act based on your truth.

❖ When your life's purpose and your personal truth are not in alignment, despite how successful you are, there's a very good chance that *you will not feel completely fulfilled.*

❖ To walk into the world of spiritual energy, you need to trust and follow divine will. The phrase *divine will* has been misused a great deal and is often misunderstood.

❖ In negative conceptions of divine will, all the power resides outside of ourselves. When we are separated from ourselves, we are separated from our spiritual energy. Accepting any of these beliefs sets us up to live our lives with our hands tied.

❖ Divine will is within us, as well as outside of us. It has nothing to do with overcoming resistance but, rather, is a force for good that helps us find our way.

❖ When you find your way, that purpose becomes your North Star. It serves as a shining destination that shields you from distorted desires along the path of your journey and reinforces what is true to you.

❖ All of the energy levels exist in relation with one another. Each liberates the others. By integrating your spiritual energy with your physical, emotional, and mental energy, you tap into huge reservoirs of additional energy awaiting within you.

# Chapter 10

# Unconditional Love for Others (Level 6)

When I began working with Ernesto, he was the CEO of one of the largest financial services institutions in Latin America; he currently heads International for Citigroup. In this role, Ernesto partners with the banking business to drive client engagement and delivery across all lines of business in Citigroup's nearly one hundred international markets. I immediately felt his energy. He was larger than life—and, frankly, a bit intimidating—exuding a magnetic charm that won you over at "hello."

Our first session took place in his office at a gorgeous palace in the center of the city. During our energy-flow session (which is what I typically call my first client session), I learned a lot about what gave Ernesto energy and what drew his energy down. In the former category, he loved to spend time with his family at their big round kitchen table, debating anything and everything, no scratch-the-surface conversations allowed. Clearly, for Ernesto and his family, debate was not just welcomed; it was a family sport. On the other side of the "energy ledger," I learned that, for Ernesto, the perception of *injustice* blocked and drained off a lot of energy, especially when he saw people who were not able to defend themselves against being mistreated.

Ernesto was passionate about life, full stop. He was straight as an arrow. *Congruency* in his life mattered; walking the talk mattered; giving unconditional love to his family, friends, and his organization mattered. Ernesto was always all in! With that emerging understanding in mind, I asked him one of my central questions: What holds you back?

He was clearly surprised by the question. He had never been asked that before, he said. Perhaps trying to buy a little time, he asked me to clarify what I meant by it. Was I talking about things like the common fear of losing a loved one to illness? No, I explained; the question tends to lead to two kinds of answers, both of which help me understand how self-aware my client is. One set of answers focuses on the things that this person is afraid of, and the other focuses on the client's beliefs—and which of these could be self-limiting.

He admitted that these were questions that he hadn't reflected much on in the past. He further acknowledged that, as a result, these were probably areas in which he didn't know that much about himself—but that he was curious. To his credit, he was a good sport and—based on his intuition—gave it a go. After a few iterations, we landed on the *fear of being rejected or being emotionally hurt* as a root cause. On the self-limiting belief side, he agreed to first address the belief that vulnerability was a weakness.

But even as he was agreeing with this assessment, Ernesto felt compelled to qualify and contradict the conclusions we had just reached. "Ricardo, I honestly don't see how these things are holding me back," he said in so many words. "I mean, I've been successful, right?"

In response, I simply asked him to trust the process and refrain from passing judgment for the time being. In the wake of this session, with his permission and help, I began a series of interviews with his work colleagues—his boss, peers, and direct reports—to develop what I think of as his professional mirror. Concurrently, I also talked to his family and friends to create the personal mirror. (Again, I always try to talk to family and friends, and that tends to be how I find out some of the most fascinating information.) With the people in both groups, I asked pretty much the same questions: What gives Ernesto energy? What takes energy away from Dad? What is he afraid of? What does he believe in?

I met Ernesto again a few weeks later for his feedback session—this time at the client's headquarters in Santa Fe, Mexico City's most prominent financial district. By now I had some thorough personal and professional mirrors mapped out and a few preliminary ideas about how the fear of rejection and the self-limiting belief about vulnerability might be holding Ernesto back. In general, I find that these kinds of feedback sessions are best approached by using the power of questions, because the answers lie within us, rather than telling him what I heard or—worse—by telling him what I thought he should do. That's the approach I took at this meeting.[1] I told Ernesto that I had a few questions I wanted to explore with him and that I truly welcomed a dialogue—even a spirited one!

So, as we sat in an elegant conference room—adorned with impressive works of art by prominent Mexican artists—I initiated a dialogue with Ernesto focused on where others saw him deriving his energy. Specifically, his team stressed that when Ernesto is doing what gives him energy, his inspiration is contagious. When Ernesto is in flow, I heard, he leads from a very special place within him. In those circumstances, team members stressed, you just simply loved the guy, and you genuinely felt safe with him, protected by him as if unconditionally loved.

Typically, this conversation is itself an energy generator because clients let their minds drift off into those spaces in their lives that give them satisfaction, even joy. The flow of the conversation is easy. The body language is relaxed and welcoming. This conversation with Ernesto was no exception: he was having fun, taking on new energy.

Inevitably, though, the conversation shifts to those things that steal energy from the client. Now the body language becomes more guarded, and the words don't flow quite as easily. Again, the feedback session with Ernesto proved no exception. And why should it have? What fun is it to talk about energy-draining situations?

And somewhere along in here, I start to introduce the notion of unintended consequences. What happens when clients are put under pressure, at work or at home, and find themselves overwhelmed by deep-seated fears? What kinds of behaviors are likely to rise to the surface? Again, I try to use questions, rather than declarations—both to spark curiosity and keep the dialogue going.

"Ernesto," I said. "Are you aware that you can come across to members of your team as very passionate when you are caught up in an argument—to the extent that the same folks who feel protected and loved by you when you're in flow can become afraid of you? As if the part of you that you lead from when you're 'in the flow' gets disconnected and you start leading from someplace else?"

It wasn't an easy question, and a long moment of reflection followed, at the end of which he focused a pair of troubled eyes on me. "Yes," he said quietly. "Yes, I can see that."

"Okay, then," I continued, seizing the moment. "Can you help me understand—if you are indeed the straight arrow that everyone thinks you are, and if you truly despise injustice as much as you say you do—why do you do it? Why do people feel so challenged by you in those situations?"

By this point, Ernesto wasn't looking me in the eye anymore. There were a few minutes of silence and of what I took to be him owning his own truth. "I don't know," he finally said.

"Would you be interested in us working together to figure out how to turn this behavior around?"

"Yes!" he exclaimed. "When can we start?"

Let's begin our exploration of Level 6 with a quick recap of the two most recent stops along our journey.

Level 4 is where your love of friends and family contributes to managing your energy. Level 5 is the realm in which your truth—in alignment with your purpose—sets you free and becomes an additional source of energy. By definition, your own personal truth and purpose are unique, and they are yours to discover. The path that leads to that discovery is equally unique and personal. As previously described, finding and following that path takes patience and discipline, in part because "defining and embodying truth"—that is, getting into alignment with life's purpose—is initially an alien concept to most of us.

I'll assume here that you made progress on Level 5 and that you're ready to move forward. The sixth level, fortunately, is not all that difficult to move toward. In fact, this one is very familiar to most of us—maybe even all of us.

At Level 6, you will learn to connect with the spiritual energy that comes from experiencing unconditional love for others outside your inner circle of friends and family.

Unconditional love is the experience of caring completely for the well-being of another person without wanting anything in return. It's the act of completely accepting them as they are.

You'll remember from earlier chapters that the unconditional love that most of us experienced in our early childhood is the pure joy that we unconsciously yearn to regain in later years. You experience hints of it far more often than you think, which explains its relative familiarity. For example, most of us are inspired by the beauty of a brilliant sunrise or sunset, right? And most of us can identify pieces of music that we find inspirational—music that inspires passion, joy, and even ecstasy. In its most powerful form—when the experience verges on the ecstatic—it taps into the same energy source as unconditional love.

What else can I say about this kind of energy? I'd point to three things:

- Again, these experiences are unique to each of us.
- You should seek to experience this kind of energy in your life, regularly. If you seek to be humane, you need to feed your soul as well as your body. It's your birthright, in a sense. Without it, part of your life will feel empty.
- Unfortunately, many people aren't aware of their need for this kind of energy. They therefore don't seek it out intentionally—and they don't celebrate it in those moments when they stumble upon it.

Letting beauty and music in to feed the soul sounds simple, easy to understand and do, and yet like in all the other levels of human energy, it is not that simple to do. I happen to be one of the lucky few who live in Marin County, California, one of the most beautiful places on Earth. Within Marin County lies Muir Woods, a majestic forest filled with some of the most impressive redwoods in the world. And deep within the woods lies a creek that springs to life during the rainy season. When it all comes together, you are in a magical forest, ready to be transported.

Why am I bringing Muir Woods into the picture, and specifically why am I being so detailed in describing its magic? Because whenever clients visit me at home, I take them there. I find that hiking in the context of natural beauty lowers people's defenses and accelerates the process of getting down to real conversations. But I also find that a beautiful setting underscores the importance of *intentionality*, mentioned in earlier chapters. Unless you establish your intention to seek and experience beauty, you'll miss it, no matter how majestic your surroundings are.[2]

This was **hard**-won knowledge. In my early explorations of experimenting with nature as a source of opening human energy, I had a pretty consistent experience. Nearly every client I took to Muir Woods proceeded through them like they were working on a checklist: *big redwood, check*; *nice creek, check*; *lush foliage, check*, while they set a pace (in "my" woods!) that made the walk feel like a competition—*keep up with me if you can*! Not surprising: most of my clients come from a world of fast-paced *doing, doing, doing*. Why should their experience at Muir Woods be any different from that?

Well, it wouldn't, unless I took responsibility for helping them understand how I wished for them to experience Muir Woods *before* they ventured in. So, toward that end, I came up with a ritual designed to help them *slow down* and *let beauty in*.

There's a long, low-slung bench at the entrance to the park. Before we enter, I ask my visitors to decide what negative energy or concerns they would like to leave there on the bench so that they can enjoy a less burdened experience in the woods. I invite them to share it with me or not—whichever they prefer. The whole ritual takes no more than five minutes, and it's worth every second of those few minutes. The checklist fades away. Their starting-out pace tends to be more measured, while their attention to beauty and expression of awe is amplified significantly. With this introduction, our visits into the woods—and into themselves—never disappoint.

## THE SECULAR AND THE SPIRITUAL

I've mentioned earlier that at the beginning of their journey toward mastering their energy, many of my clients shy away from the word *spirituality*. By and large, they do so because they believe that as the leader of a secular organization—a corporation—they have no right to impose their own beliefs on others. I understand this reluctance and agree with it, as far as it goes.

Yes, it's a tricky balance, and in some cultures even more so than in others. We certainly don't want our companies being dogmatic in a heavy-handed way that excludes individuals or groups. On the other hand, we don't want those companies actively denying that spirituality may help foster a culture that creates humane leaders. To deprive the organization of spiritual energy also risks depriving it of emotional energy—and that leaves only physical and mental energy.

These last two kinds of energy are valuable, of course, but they're not sufficient. In the wake of the COVID pandemic, many corporate leaders wondered why even some of their most productive and motivated workers were declining to return to work. My explanation? The pandemic revealed, in a stark sort of way, that most organizations today offer *only* physical and mental challenges and rewards. Without seeing a spiritual or emotional reason to go back into the workplace, many people simply didn't.

So, on the corporate level, the best we can hope for is to strike something like the right balance between the secular and the spiritual—or, looking at it from a different lens, between rigor and caring. We need to acknowledge that striking this balance is not an easy task and that it's one of the things that separates the merely good leader from the great one. In my work, therefore, I encourage my clients to tackle the issue of spirituality in the workplace head-on and to keep thinking about it in as nuanced a way as possible.

In other words, *keep it complex*. Keep finding ways to let the organization be both powerful and loving.

Finding allies that can help you hold your mirror—as you are experimenting your way to finding the balance within the rigor/care energy polarity—is essential. Perhaps your partner in human resources can help. I have to say that most professionals in that field really get what I am writing about in this book and see the benefits of how your personal work can positively contribute to the growth of you and the business.

I was very moved when Mike, the head of human resources of one of my clients, asked me how he could be of help to his boss in her development plan. I thanked him for reaching out and asked him how he was experiencing her. He shared how much she had changed since we'd been working together, but he candidly said that, at times, she returned to her old-and-cold transactional ways of interacting with people, thereby creating confusion: *Who do we have today—Ms. Jekyll or Ms. Hyde?* I thanked Mike for his candor, and asked him, "What do you think is the right thing to do?"

He reflected for a moment and replied, "Well, my job is to support her in becoming the leader that she wants to be."

"And how do you think you can do that?"

"I need to be honest with her," he responded, "and point out when she shows up as Ms. Hyde, right?"

This time I chose to affirm. "Yes, Mike, that feels right. You're with her every day, and your guidance on the spot will probably turn out to be an amazing support for her as she tries to evolve into an effective *and* caring leader." In effect, my client would have an amazing sparring partner—a supporter, as she acted on her desire to change.

This isn't pie-in-the-sky stuff; it's a savvy HR professional trying to advance a common cause. It's good business!

I wish there were a Mike everywhere I work. If for some reason a strong HR resource isn't available to you, look elsewhere for allies who will help you enable the organization to strike the right balance—that is, being both powerful and loving. Identify the people who truly care about your success and who will keep you honest as you set out to strike that balance.

## SPIRITUAL ENERGY WITHIN A LEADER

In many cases, initiating a discussion like the one above is how I steer a client conversation into the realm of what might be called the spiritual energy within a leader. I start in the safe (but complex!) realm of the corporation and work my way in toward the person across the desk from me.

"Tom," I might say, "having talked about the company and the kind of supportive environment you want to encourage here, now I want to talk about *you*. How open are you to giving yourself permission to add spiritual energy into your journey?"

This is almost always an awkward moment. Most of my clients don't like it the first time they hear me talking about it. Some of them simply don't get what I mean by "spiritual energy." Others get it—or think they get it—but tell me flat out that they don't see how complicating their development journey with issues of spirituality is going to help with their leadership skills or their efforts to manage their energy levels.

Whenever it seems appropriate, I persist. I answer their questions and ask questions back. I try connecting the dots in new ways. I talk about joy in their lives and their experience of unconditional love and the benefits that come from trying to connect to this bliss as a way to finding a genuine connection with others outside their inner circle, perhaps their teams. I ask them to think about the energy that's associated with those wonderful moments—and encourage them to speculate about what would happen if they could bring that kind of energy to bear on their role as a leader.

It doesn't often go quickly, and the timing has to be right. (You can't give to others when they're not ready to receive.) I can't point to a lot of "road to Damascus" conversion experiences on the spiritual side of my professional work. But in most cases, we eventually get to a place where my clients are interested and engaged in the conversation—and at that point, I ask for their permission to move forward and explore this energy. This is important. It's a door that may only be opened once in these busy people's lives. If they aren't on board, the exploration won't go well, and the effort will fail, and my client may well wind up reaching exactly the wrong conclusion: *just as I suspected—spiritual energy is not for me.*

A terrible lesson!

Spiritual energy is for everyone who is open to accessing it. It's our birthright and an additional source of energy in your life, which may become accessible just when your physical and mental energy are nearing exhaustion.

## WHY MAKE THE EFFORT?

Accepting and integrating spiritual energy is about embracing the mystery of life. It's about deciding to dive into the river and go with the flow.[3] You can't complete your full development within the human energy field—you can't overcome what's holding you back in its entirety and move forward in a decisive way—unless you acknowledge that you fit into a bigger picture, including a more embracing view of humanity.

As I've already explained, spiritual energy is a critical ingredient in managing your energy. Does that sound like I'm mixing up the mundane and the sublime? Yes, I am. Purposefully. Take it a step further: What would happen if you tried to make bread without yeast? You might get *something*, but it wouldn't be bread.[4] I think of spiritual energy as the yeast in the bread of human energy.

You'll recall that we've talked (at Level 4) about loving your family and friends in a purposeful way. At Level 6, we talked about the experience of unconditional love, both for yourself and for others outside your inner circle. This means that we care completely for the well-being of another person without wanting anything in return for it—without any conditions— and while being completely accepting of them as they are. Now I'm talking about extending this kind of love to *far broader circles*.

It takes courage to do this, especially in the context of a materialistic culture. But if you think about it, your self comes from the same place, in the same condition, as everybody else's. By that I mean that *everyone has a part of them that is the same as that part of you* and that is just as good as (and no better than) that part of you. If this reflection is difficult for you to accept, then perhaps thinking about it in the following way helps (as discussed before): you are born with your heart completely full and your head completely empty. Your full heart is the same as any other newborn's heart.

It's as important to feed our souls as it is to feed our bodies.[5] When our souls aren't fed, we become cynical about existence. Our lives start to feel like one hurdle after another, and we lack any sense of well-being. Sometimes we try to overcome that something-is-missing feeling with material wealth—only to find that this doesn't work. In truth, the only way to fill this kind of void, and derive this kind of energy, is through Level 6–type experiences.

What does this mean? It means devoting *time* and *energy* to this part of ourselves in our daily lives. For each of us, this translates into something different. It may mean adding an intentional mantra in our regular meditation.[6] It may also mean solo treks in the mountains or silent walks on the beach. It may mean listening to the type of music that takes you to a blissful place. But for all of us, it's about devoting time and focus to this purpose. When you do this regularly, you will awaken vast parts of yourself that are full of beauty and love that you will get to know, and they will become part of your "normal you." You will learn to accept people just as they are—standing in honor and respect for who they are, welcoming their differences from yours, and supporting them as they move toward their own version of excellence. When you achieve this kind of deep experience at the sixth level, your teams, peers, community, and society will all benefit.

## WHAT'S IN IT FOR OTHERS?

This raises an important question on a practical level: What's in it for others? Do leaders seeking humane-leader relationships with their teams really have to take this on?

I say yes because this is where the team's energy lives. When you start to see everybody on your team as fundamentally similar to each other *at the essence*, inherent biases start to go out your window, and diversity of thought starts to come in your front door. Paradoxically, you are free—perhaps for the first time—to stop surrounding yourself with people who are exactly like you. You are free to embrace people who think differently. You start to make space for others and for teams of others to take root and flourish.

"Ricardo," I hear you saying, "this all sounds very lofty and inspirational, but again—what's in it for the company?"

It's a good question, which I'll answer indirectly. One of my clients is a CEO whom I'll call Suzie. She cares deeply about the hundred thousand–plus people in her company, and she also cares about the other five million people that her organization is arguably responsible for—ranging from agricultural workers to truck drivers to maintenance crews and cafeteria workers under contract. At the beginning of her journey, Suzie insisted that she was not a "spiritual person." I told her that she was one of the most spiritual people I knew. How so? It seemed to me that her unconditional love for her community and society was second to none and that if she were more conscious of this, her work on Level 6 could be quite a joyous experience.

What's in it for the company? *Collective purpose*, and the shared energy that grows out of that purpose. Remember my earlier comment about motivated people not coming back to work after the first waves of the COVID pandemic subsided? This is the ground I was talking about.

Beginning about a decade ago, Suzie's organization decided to commit itself to advancing the cause of human rights on a global scale. Not long afterward, the company earned a perfect score on the Human Rights Campaign Foundation's Corporate Equality Index. Could they have done so without a strong, shared sense of purpose, reinforced from above? I would say, *doubtful*.

Suzie was not the first CEO at her organization to embrace purpose, but she certainly found ways to expand and intensify the effort. From the vantage point of an interested observer, this looks like a kind of joy that very, very few people beyond the age of toddlerhood get to enjoy. If you're looking for a compelling reason to take that CEO job when it's offered to you, this might be it!

That said, you don't have to be in charge of a hundred thousand–plus people to be energized through your exercise of spirituality in the workplace. Let's say you're a middle manager who's responsible for twenty people. If you love your team, they're probably going to love you back. And they're going to trust you, and they're going to tell you the truth, and you're going to get better insights from data with which you can make better decisions—incidentally saving you so much of that *time* you've been longing for!—and gradually create a kind of energy that you probably haven't experienced for many, many years.

I've tried in this chapter to bring together the sublime and the mundane in a persuasive way. Can you be a spiritual being at work? Should you be—and if so, why? How do you benefit as an individual, and how does that benefit your coworkers and your organization?

In the next chapter, I sharpen the focus on the sublime and how and where it intersects most tellingly with the work of the humane leader.

## YOUR HOMEWORK FOR LEVEL 6

Within this chapter, my analyses and prescriptions are related to connecting to the unconditional love within us, so that from that place, we can seek to connect with others.

A key question to ask yourself at Level 6:
Can I be open, curious, and nonjudgmental as I learn about what holds me back from experiencing unconditional love for others, outside of my inner circle of friends and family?

## SOME INTENTIONS TO SET FOR YOURSELF AT LEVEL 6

### Set the intention to feed your soul.

- What helps you experience bliss? Music? A sunrise?
- When was the last time you intentionally looked for an experience that would lead you to feeling blissful? How often do you do that? (Do you *ever* do it?)

- Remember: feeding the soul is essential to achieving a balanced level of energy.

## Set the intention to balance rigor and care as a way to bring unconditional love into your life.

- On a scale of 1 to 10, with 1 being "balance is missing" and 10 being "I'm happy with my balance," rate yourself. Are you aware of how you balance rigor and care? Are you good at it? If not, what's holding you back? Become curious about your response.
- Remember that rigor without care is brutal. Remember, too, that care without rigor can't hold its power—it becomes too fluffy and gets taken for granted.
- Without this balance, the people around you—in your family and at work—won't feel safe, and you won't feel safe.
- Conversely, with proper balance and spiritual energy, unconditional love for others can be attained.

## Set the intention to unconditionally love every human being.

- This is about achieving connecting to self, so that from this place, you can experience others in you and vice versa. It's a marathon, not a sprint.
- As in the previous chapter, bringing spiritual energy into your life must be *experienced*. If you try to accomplish it vicariously—for example, through a series of questions and answers alone—you will fall short in your spiritual energy growth.
- Here's an end-of-chapter exercise. Think of someone you find despicable. If only for a minute or two, think about why the person strikes you that way. Now try to

imagine something buried deep inside that person that is exactly like something buried somewhere inside you and is also buried somewhere inside the person that you love the most in this world. (Visualize your significant other or your kids or whatever works for you.) I'm not talking organs and body parts—although it's interesting to consider, on a purely physical level, how very much alike we all are. Instead, I'm talking about *self*, about the person's *essence*.

Take more than a few minutes for this part of the exercise. It's important. If you can reach that place in your imagination, you can start to forgive that person for being trapped in that despicable shell—and you're on your way to truly loving others unconditionally. By almost any measure, you're already far freer than that person is, right? Doesn't that allow you to view that (seemingly) despicable person with compassion, rather than with hate or anger? When you do so, you move your energy to a different place—with very real benefits for you.

How open are you to believing that there is a similar individuated spark in all of us?

Do you see anyone in your family and in your work as sharing this spark in all of us? If not, why? What is holding you back?

Can you be a spiritual being at work? If so, how—and if not, why? This is important to know.

## THE TAKEAWAYS

❖ At Level 6, you learn to connect with the spiritual energy that comes from experiencing unconditional love for others outside your inner circle of friends and family.

❖ Unconditional love is the experience of caring for the well-being of another person without wanting anything in return. It's the act of completely accepting them exactly as they are.

❖ The unconditional love that most of us experienced in our early childhood is the pure joy that we unconsciously yearn to regain in later years.

❖ You probably experience it far more often than you think, and in its most powerful form. When the experience verges on the ecstatic, it taps into the same energy source as unconditional love (that is, a breath-taking sunrise).

❖ We should *all* seek to experience this kind of energy in our lives, regularly. If we seek to be humane, we need to feed our souls as well as our bodies. It's our birthright, in a sense. Without it, part of our lives will feel empty.

❖ Bringing spiritual energy into a corporate context requires a tricky balancing act. It is the right thing not to impose your beliefs on others, while being open to integrating spiritual energy as part of the human energy repertoire enabling the development of humane leaders.

❖ Tackle the issue of spirituality in the workplace head-on, and keep thinking about it in as nuanced a way as possible. Keep finding ways to let the organization be both powerful and loving.

❖ Finding allies that can help you hold your mirror as you are experimenting your way to finding the balance within the rigor and care energy polarity is essential.

❖ Accepting and integrating spiritual energy is about embracing the mystery of life. You can't overcome in its entirety what's holding you back unless you acknowledge that you fit into a bigger picture, including a more embracing view of humanity.

## Chapter 11

# Seeking the Greater Universal Pattern (Level 7)

Not so long ago, Laura—the chief people officer of a Fortune 100 organization—sent me a note that opened with a few welcome words of thanks but then moved on to an expression of concern:

> Ricardo, our chairman is very pleased with the progress of our CEO succession, but there is one emerging roadblock. Our current CEO, James—whom I think you know—appears to be having difficulty in letting go, and we don't know what to do. He is without a hint of a doubt a good person. But in his relationships with the internal candidates to succeed him, James is exerting an unnecessary amount of pressure. If he continues behaving this way, there's a high risk of some of them quitting before the end of the year, forcing us to go look externally. I understand there is no magic wand here but would much appreciate if you could help James go back to the place where he was—the self-confident leader who is ready to retire—so we can all happily celebrate his retirement when the time comes, along with his appointed successor. Is that possible?

Working with Laura was always a pleasure, and I appreciated the way she was approaching this new challenge. She understood that my role was not to *convince* James of anything; my role was to help him figure out what part of his life story was holding him back, unconsciously, from letting go. Fortunately, there was plenty of time to work with James on the task of managing his energy to lead from self.

"Yes, Laura," I wrote back. "I think it's possible, and it'll be a privilege to work closely with James. Let me know when we can start."

We got started, and working with James was a pure joy. He is indeed a good person—humble, with high integrity and convictions. I honestly couldn't detect any misplaced ego getting in the way, especially when he confirmed his intention to work with me in a way that would be totally aligned with the organization's goals. "I am ready to retire, Ricardo," he emphasized once he got the gist of my mandate. "Honest I am! But I want to prepare my potential successors as best I can, so the company has the best possible situation moving forward. I want to retire honorably and, in the years to come, focus on board work and serving my country."

To my delight, James already had an intuitive understanding of intentional energy. He took great care of his physical energy (Level 1), sleeping an average of seven hours a day and working out every other day, following a routine that required the discipline of an athlete. Alternate days were for meditation and prayer. He had clarity on the power of quality breathing and combined it with a balanced diet. I just offered a minor tweak, helping him integrate the intention to feel pleasure into his daily physical rituals. For James, the shift of energy from managing a daily checklist of activities to feeling joy when taking good care of himself began to create space in his ability to feel.

Most of the work we did was at Level 2. James was awesome at taking care of others but discovered that he was controlling to a fault. As he confessed to me, "I never realized that I am constantly looking for perfection in everything."

Using the Internal Family Systems framework described in chapter 3, James began to recognize his deep longing to *belong*. There was a young part of him that desperately needed to be seen as worthy of being loved, while another part—the Protector, as we called it—made sure that this younger, vulnerable facet was not exposed. This Protector turned out to be quite stubborn, and for very good reasons. James's upbringing was very tough, although not without a certain kind of love—a combination of circumstances that I've agreed to keep confidential. But given this unusual challenge, I brought in a Family Constellation expert, who helped me untangle a couple of key family disorders (Level 4) that, once ordered, created space for James to understand that he was good enough—*more* than good enough!—to close the Love of Self gap significantly.

James was quite pleased, albeit surprised, by the findings. "I pride myself on being quite self-aware and in control of my emotions," he said at one point, "but these findings and practices are surprising me and—I have to say—changing my life for the better!"

That was the good news. The bad news was that when I next talked to Laura, she reported, to my surprise, that while James obviously was in better spirits, his behavior with his subordinates—the strong internal candidates—was showing no improvement. I thanked her for the candid feedback and thought through my approach and our progress to date. I continued to believe that once James mastered his energy, he would be able to gain freedom of choice in his behaviors.

It was time to focus on Level 3: that is, to focus on surfacing his self-limiting belief system. But that wasn't easy. James treated his belief system almost as a Book of Law—as something not to be tempered with, to avoid the risk of losing his principles. So I chose instead to jump to Level 7, in an effort to connect James with his spiritual energy. The notion of connecting with his spirituality seemed potentially appealing. He loved music and poetry, and sometimes on our rambles outdoors, he'd stop to smell a wildflower to ascertain if it had a scent. Given that trait, we also worked on the *intention* to seek and experience beauty, to nurture his soul. This seemed to move him deeply, as did the challenge of exploring his purpose: *Why was he here?*

One day, while we were enjoying lunch together, I introduced James to a mantra that I learned from Eva Pierrakos—see chapter 8—and which guides me in my daily meditation:

> I commit to accept the will of the Universe, with all my heart and all my soul.
> I deserve the best in life.
> I serve the best cause in life.
> I am a divine manifestation of the Universe.

James thought about this for a few minutes. I could see that he was deeply moved, and he responded by saying something to the effect of, "If we are all the same, and we should be loving each other unconditionally, and I pride myself on serving the right cause, then who am I to challenge the will of the Universe?" In other words, despite the high and thick walls of his belief system, there was curiosity and an openness to explore, and Level 7 gave him the space to finally soften.

At that point, I brought up the idea first introduced to me by Scott Coady: to center your spiritual energy, you need to surrender to the mystery of life. "Wow," he said, "that feels so right!" I admit that I'm finding it hard to reconstruct this scene in a way that lets you follow along emotionally. But here's the truth: James felt so liberated by the idea of surrendering to the energy at this level that he broke down in tears.

Once he recalibrated his spiritual awareness to accommodate *surrender*, his need to control significantly softened. In his own time, James came to the realization that he was holding the internal candidates to an unreasonable standard of perfection. Ultimately, his ability to let go—thereby giving the organization the opportunity to have a succession choice and giving him the chance to retire in a way that satisfied everyone—was inspiring. And, as James told me at one of our last sessions, he felt like he had tapped into a limitless source of energy and was ready to take on new worlds.

Level 7 is the final step in understanding and feeling the human energy field. It is about *achieving serenity and, while in it, being able to have pure creative thoughts*. It is about understanding the perfect pattern of creation and being at ease with that understanding.

So, at this point in the conversation, as you can imagine, my clients who are not as spiritually aware as James was—those for whom spiritual energy is a faraway concept—start to demand simultaneous translation, like at the United Nations. *What is this guy talking about?* Depending on the specifics of the situation, I may try to engage them in a dialogue that goes something like the following:

ME: We've already agreed that you're a curious and engaged observer of the human condition, right?

CLIENT: *(hesitantly)* Yes . . .

ME: Okay. So, for a few minutes, I want you to think about a couple of questions that I'm going to ask you. But understand ahead of time that I'm not going to ask you to tell me whatever answers you come up with. Okay?

CLIENT: *(looking a little off balance)* Okay.

ME: Good. So here are three questions—keep it simple, just a few words that come to you: Why do we exist? What's our purpose for being here? If you have a soul, what is that soul supposed to accomplish? Again: think for a few minutes, and let me know when you're done.

CLIENT: *(after a few minutes, still off balance)* Okay. Done.

ME: So now my question to you is, did asking yourself those questions make you feel happy or fearful? Was the feeling you were experiencing as you thought about your answers closer to joy or to dread?

Often, my clients locate themselves closer to the fearful/dreadful end of the spectrum. I quickly reassure them that that's not something to be embarrassed about or even surprised by. Not so long ago, I would have answered the joy/dread question the same way: "I want creation to make sense—I want it to have a purpose—but I'm afraid it doesn't." And that's one of the things that, at least in my mind, dredges up the dread.

I've already argued that we're all made out of the same universal essence. The question on the table is, where did all that essence *come* from, and what's it supposed to be *used* for?

These kinds of questions don't lend themselves to easy answers. Scott Coady's wisdom, introduced in earlier chapters, basically was that *the way to center yourself through the mystery of life is just to surrender to it*. But a lot of the people I serve don't *like* to surrender to mysteries, right? They like to *challenge* and *solve* mysteries. "When you start to talk about the greater universal pattern and the mystery of life," a somewhat frustrated client once said to me, "I get a rash."

This kind of reaction reminds me that it's my responsibility to keep these conversations translatable to the business context—or, as others would say, somewhere near ground level. Again: Why bother pursuing answers to mysteries that don't have easy answers?

There's a famous Sigmund Freud quote that may or may not be real. Supposedly, he said that the measure of a healthy person was *the ability to love and to work*. Now, the closest anyone has come to quoting Freud directly along those lines is a recollection by a fellow Viennese psychoanalyst named Richard Sterba, who asked Freud how Sterba and his colleagues should try to motivate people to undergo analysis, which after all is a long, costly, and difficult process. Freud responded that psychotherapists should simply point out that they offer their patients relief from their symptoms, an increase in their working capacity, and an improvement in their personal and social relationships.[1]

In other words, the healer/guide/coach should work back from desired destinations and explain that *this particular journey will get us there*. So, when I hit this mystery-of-life roadblock with a client, I dutifully try that. And in many cases—even most cases—I still meet resistance. Why is that? I'm guessing that those people, like so many of us, had some sort of bad experience with an organized belief system at some point in their life. Today, they are convinced that any such belief system is more likely to reduce their freedom of choice than enhance it.

I get that, and I don't disagree. On the other hand . . . I think that many of us want to understand how we fit into something bigger. We want to understand if all of us, with all of our imperfections, somehow add up to something perfect. That *yearning* that we humans can't seem to get away from—

what *is* it? Is it there just to drive us crazy, or might it be yet another door to yet another source of energy?

I say it's the latter.

## IMPERFECT IS PERFECT

On the seventh level, we find our reason for being. When we're in a balanced state of experiencing success and bliss, we are in a state of clarity, in which we understand that *everything is perfect the way it is*, even when it is imperfect.

Though for James it required no further explanation, for most of us, it's time to go back to the United Nations for some more simultaneous translation: What is Ricardo talking about now? Well, I tell my clients, curious people like to seek out and fix problems. What would they do all day if there were no imperfections in the world—what would they fix? They would be like sled dogs with no sleds and no snow. And on a more exalted plane: What if we ourselves and everyone around us were already perfect? How would we learn the art of perfecting things? How would we learn to love under perfect conditions?

This is the lesson of that truly despicable person I described in the previous chapter whom I challenged you to attempt to love. Now we're upgrading that experience of broadening our love from that one sad person to all of humanity.

Wait a minute (I hear): love *everybody*? Yes, I say. This is not your obligation but your birthright. It's the natural state we all had when we were born—when we came into this world and, as I said before, when our hearts were completely full and our minds completely empty and we were fully present in the pure bliss of the moment.

"But why bother pursuing this birthright?" they ask. "That sounds unattainable." I respond that I know it sounds like that, but it's worth pursuing if you are up for exploring a journey toward a truly gratifying destination—in these pages and in life. The more we allow ourselves access to this energy, the more alive we become and the more human we become—and the more energy we get back.

And, ultimately, it makes us more humane leaders. Shakti Gawain, mentioned in earlier chapters, talks about a universe that is fundamentally good and constantly changing. If she's right, that argues for making every effort to *share* the goodness of the universe. This isn't necessarily selfless, she says: "As we give out our energy, we make space for more to flow into us."[2]

If that's true—and I think it is—then the "burden of leadership" that so many CEOs and leaders complain about is a clear case of upside-down thinking. Being in a position to be a humane leader on *those* lofty heights is not a burden but, truly, a gift to be savored. And like everything that makes more space inside of us, it means more access to our essence and our energy.

## A PAUSE TO SUM UP

At this point in my clients' journey toward becoming a humane leader, I tend to hear one of two things. The members of one group—happily, the larger group—tell me that they feel inspired to try mastering their energy and want to start experiencing the benefits I'm describing *right away*.

But then there are the members of the other group, who confess to feeling a little overwhelmed and want to go back and explore mastering their energy within the first four levels before they move in this deep. I honor this level of awareness. As I said before, follow your energy and things happen for a reason; in due time, after you explore the first four levels, you may decide to take the plunge and explore the rest.

Meanwhile, you may still feel stuck in a time-management mindset: How can I carve out time to learn to master my energy when I'm already hard up for free time?

Well, a small investment of time leads to a large harvest of energy—and that in turn begets more energy, which in turn positions you to be a humane leader. This isn't the best analogy, but picture one of those movies you've seen about race cars flying around on an oval track somewhere. Sure, the drivers and their teams know that if they could just go *flat out for the entire race without stopping*, they would win. But that's not real. So they pull over at the right intervals, get all four tires switched out, and gas up.[3] I still say, *master your energy, not your time*. But certainly, invest the time needed to learn how to master your energy.

Energy follows energy. What I am offering is a challenging but balanced approach to human energy awareness. Level 1—having a felt sense of simple physical pleasure—is a pretty straightforward jumping-off point. Level 7, which we've just been exploring, is anything but simple, for the reasons I've explained. Between those two bookends, we have a purposeful pattern of alternation. Levels 2, 4, and 6 focus on emotional energy—that is, energy dominated by our desires. Levels 3 and 5 inject rationality—that is, understanding situations in a clear way and speaking and following your truth.

I bring this up to underscore a compelling truth: energy can be sought out in almost every dimension of our human experience. Again, energy follows energy.

This brings us to the end of our seven-level journey of the human energy field. As you've seen, it's a journey focused on *being*. It's a journey that draws on your past to help you shape yourself into a humane leader in the present—and to open new opportunities for becoming a humane leader in your future.

In that spirit, our next and last chapter focuses on *becoming*. What new doors do you want to open, and where do you want your new paths to take you?

## YOUR HOMEWORK FOR LEVEL 7

In this chapter, my analyses and prescriptions all focus on connecting to your reason for being and—from that place—sourcing your creative thoughts.

A key question to ask yourself at Level 7:
Can I be open, curious, and nonjudgmental about what holds me back from surrendering to the mystery of life?

## SOME INTENTIONS TO SET FOR YOURSELF AT LEVEL 7

### Set the intention to surrender to the mystery of life.

- On a scale of 1 to 10, with 1 being closed and 10 being open, rate yourself on how open you are to surrendering to the mystery of life. Speak the truth here. What experiences get in your way? Make a list and reflect on it. What are you afraid of? Why do you have this limiting belief?

### Set the intention to connect divine will (Level 5), divine love (Level 6), and divine mind (Level 7).

- What do you feel if you hear "imperfection is perfection"? Reflect on this question from a *felt* sense—in other words, do I feel anxious or uncomfortable? Or do I feel peaceful and liberated?

- How would we learn to love ourselves and others under perfect conditions?
- What gets in your way of accepting that, as humans, we are imperfect beings?
- Why do we hold ourselves to such levels of perfection?
- By connecting our freedom of choice with unconditional love for ourselves and others, we open the door to unlimited self-compassion and unlimited creative power (clarity of thought).

**Set the intention of being both successful and blissful.**

As I shared in the previous chapter, bringing spiritual energy into your life must be experienced, and thus doing it through just a series of questions will fall short in your spiritual energy growth.

Let me give you the same challenge that I gave to James over lunch, as described above. I handed him a written copy of a mantra that I learned from Eva Pierrakos and asked him to ponder it. I'll repeat it here:

> I commit to accept the will of the Universe, with all my heart and all my soul.
> I deserve the best in life.
> I serve the best cause in life.
> I am a divine manifestation of the Universe.

- Read it three times, out loud, and slowly. Really allow it to go into you. Feel each sentence, and ask yourself, *What part of this mantra speaks to me? What part of this mantra is not me?*

- Get out your journal and *work through it*, word by word and line and line. Everyone's reaction is different. Some people connect with the first sentence but feel that the second one is self-serving. Others think that the last sentence is too arrogant. Where are you? Be curious, because this may help you distinguish between what gets in the way of centering your spiritual energy and what is already accepted or in the process of being accepted. Again, this is all good to know.
- There is no conflict between being intentional with your spiritual energy and your mental, physical, and emotional energy. You can be very successful and very blissful at the same time!

## THE TAKEAWAYS

- Level 7 is about *achieving serenity and, while in it, being able to have pure creative thoughts*. It is about understanding the perfect pattern of creation and being at ease with that understanding.
- To center your spiritual energy, you need to surrender to the mystery of life.
- Surrendering—letting go—creates coherence for you to fully tap into your limitless source of energy.
- When we're in a balanced state of experiencing success and bliss, we are in a state of clarity, in which we understand that *everything is perfect the way it is*—even when it is imperfect.

- ❖ Being in a position to be a humane leader at the pinnacle of a large human organization is not a burden but a gift to be savored. And like everything that makes more space inside of us, it means more access to our essence and our energy.
- ❖ Energy can be sought out in almost every dimension of our human experience. *Energy follows energy.*

# Epilogue: The Journey Continues

In 1949, an American author and teacher named Joseph Campbell published a book called *The Hero with a Thousand Faces*. His premise was that there's a single heroic myth across all human cultures. The heroes at the center of all those myths and legends embark on a journey—and the conditions, phases, and outcomes of that journey, says Campbell, are remarkably consistent, because they grow out of our shared human psyche.[1]

That's why they're so powerful: they land squarely in our collective unconscious. The hero is called to go seek out a treasure, resists, but finally gives in to that call, gets in and out of a lot of tough scrapes—often with the help of a supernatural mentor figure, whom Campbell calls the "Old Man"—secures the treasure, and returns home a much-changed person, eager to share what they've learned along the way. Think Jonah, Odysseus, Huck Finn, and the Karate Kid. Think *Aladdin*, *Star Wars*, and *The Lion King*. Think Frodo and Gandalf in the *Rings* trilogy: only the most recent example, although it's one that hews very close to Campbell's typology.

*The Hero with a Thousand Faces* was well received when it was first released, and it has gradually achieved classic status. It has been translated into more than twenty languages and has sold more than a million copies. That's not to say it's an easy read—it definitely isn't. But it's worth digging into. Ultimately, Campbell describes a heroic path of constant deaths and rebirths, at the center of which is the Mystery of Life.

I was first introduced to Joseph Campbell's work when I joined the faculty of the Executive Breakthrough Program, led by Erica Ariel Fox.[2] I became fascinated with Campbell's philosophy. As I read him, there are really only two possible responses: to run away from the Mystery or to accept and embrace it. But it turns out that running away is really not a workable response because it involves sticking our heads in the sand and oversimplifying our lives to the point of making them meaningless. The only workable response, therefore, is to be open to life and to accept all that it puts in front of us—joy and pain, success and failure—and to *keep working at it*. We need to live alongside the Mystery, and even learn to embrace it. We need to accept the fact that there's probably a Coauthor to our personal story, probably with a bigger pen than our own, and yet keep trying to write that story.

The hero's journey is summarized in Figure 2. Note that the hero travels from the known (consciousness) to the unknown (unconsciousness). There are regular interventions along the way by supernatural forces and Threshold Guardians ("Old Men") and various other sorts of mentors and helpers. Nevertheless, after crossing the Threshold into the unknown, the hero inevitably steers toward a fundamental crisis—the Abyss—which ultimately results metaphorically in death and rebirth, to gain revelation and transformation. Then comes atonement for sins and mistakes in the hero's past and—at long last—a return to the known, which includes the responsibility to share with the tribe what was learned.

I want to bring the hero's journey home to my own work. The clients I work with have gotten a call to adventure, often in the form of a promotion that is either proposed or a fait

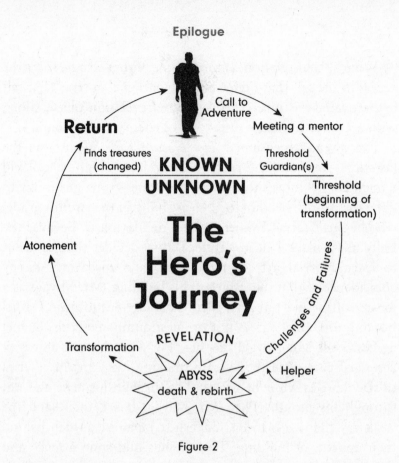

Figure 2

accompli, often in the form of desire to become a larger version of themselves. They now have to undertake their own epic journey: a journey inward. My job is to help them out along the way—although I'm squarely in Joseph Campbell's "Old Man" model rather than in the supernatural helper/magician camp. I start them on their path from the known (or conscious) psyche to the unknown (or unconscious) psyche, letting them know that's it's likely to be a bumpy ride, almost certainly involving hard work, grief, and struggle. I don't use words like *abyss*, *death*, and *rebirth*, but I tell them that they're going to have to let a part of themselves go: their fears and the self-limiting beliefs that lie behind those psychological walls. I warn them that it's often painful.

What's the revelation on the far side of that struggle? It's the access to the self that I referred to in earlier chapters. That self is discovered—is given birth—in the revelation phase, along with access to immense reservoirs of energy and wisdom.

I've already mentioned *The Karate Kid*. When was the last time you saw it? Briefly, a New Jersey high school kid named Daniel moves to LA and picks the wrong girl to try to date: the ex-girlfriend of the biggest bully in the twelfth grade, who begins beating Daniel up on a regular basis. Because the bully has a black belt in karate, Daniel decides that he needs to learn martial arts to fight back, and discovers—happy coincidence!—that the janitor in his building, Mr. Miyagi, is a master of the martial arts. Mr. Miyagi agrees to train Daniel but only if Daniel agrees not to question his methods. Daniel agrees. First Mr. Miyagi has his new student wash and wax a row of cars until they gleam, moving his arms in a series of wide circles while he breathes in through his nose and out through his mouth. Then Mr. Miyagi has Daniel sand the walkway that leads to his makeshift Japanese garden behind their apartment building. Then he has him stain a fence and then paint a house—in all cases, following specific prescribed physical and breathing movements.

Finally, Daniel rebels against this seemingly pointless grunt work. But it turns out that the physical and mental discipline involved in these apparently menial tasks are the first steps toward facing down his nemesis in a karate championship. Further instruction—like learning to keep one's balance in a rollover-prone rowboat—follows. I won't give away the ending, of course.

Why cite the story of *The Karate Kid* here, this late in the book? I often recount this plot to my clients when I feel them getting confused—when the journey is getting rough, and I'm starting to hear, once again, questions like, "I get the personal gain of doing this self-discovery journey, Ricardo, but what does this have to do with work?" When Daniel snaps at Mr. Miyagi, claiming that his teacher has simply been using him to get a series of unpleasant household chores out of the way, Mr. Miyagi asks Daniel to demonstrate wax-on, and wax-off, and so on. When the skeptical Daniel does so, Mr. Miyagi starts to throw punches at him—and to Daniel's great surprise, he is able to go toe-to-toe with his master.

It is not until that very moment that Daniel is able to *feel* what he has already learned. By being able to defend himself against Mr. Miyagi's assault, he finds that he is able to let go of his thoughts, fears, and self-limiting beliefs and just be in the moment, *in the zone and flow*, based on his newly acquired skills. It is then that he believes that he actually has a chance to win.

Whenever I share this story, it is with the intention of integrating back into the workplace the learnings of my client's journey of self-discovery—that is, the learning gained by working in all seven layers within the human energy field. It is with the goal of helping my client move from trying to understand things rationally to trying to accept things emotionally. Most of the time, it works—maybe because most of my clients were young when *The Karate Kid* opened and were inspired by it. Or maybe it's the pure power of storytelling through the lens of the hero's journey, which connects us to our collective unconscious.

If it still doesn't resonate with you, then pick another story. Yoda training Luke in *The Empire Strikes Back* is a good one.[3] Because we're talking about the collective unconscious here, there's a story out there somewhere that will inspire you and help you believe that it is worth making the necessary effort in Levels 1 through 7. It *is* worth making that effort.

Actually, this is where having very ambitious and very *driven* clients works to our shared advantage: even though they could easily give up the quest and turn around to walk back to the Known with no obvious consequences, they almost never do—even when the discipline at hand feels odd or silly or begins to get a little painful. By and large, they keep moving forward. The incremental energies they gain, as they progress from Levels 1 through 7, help keep them motivated.

And finally, they succeed. Welcome back, heroes! Welcome aboard, humane leaders!

## FROM "WHY AM I HERE?" TO "WHERE DO I WANT TO GO NEXT?"

Much of this book has been about learning how to master your energy to complement and gain access to sources of energy beyond the physical and the mental. If you learn to master your energy, there is no need to be concerned about your time. You experience the benefits of being present in the moment by pursuing certain disciplines to tap into and master your energy. Why do we care about mastering our energy? The first and easy answer is, *so we'll have more of it*. And, by extension, with additional energy we'll have more time, which ideally we'll use to do more of what gives us energy. Of course, we can't manufacture more minutes in the hour or hours in the day—but when we get access to our inner energy, those terrible constraints in us that affected our time management seem to loosen. We're in the zone, in the flow. We can do much more than we ever did before and feel more fulfilled while doing it.

The second and less easy answer is, *we master our energy so that we can change ourselves*. How does this happen? Mastering our energy gives us access to our true selves—a concept that I introduced in earlier chapters. In the simplest terms, by mastering our energy, we change our personalities. We become our better selves. And we *lead* from this new place, with confidence and compassion, with empathy and humanity. We become the humane leaders that we set out to be at the beginning of this journey.

"Self" is where your creative power lives. It's an unlimited energy source, which manifests even to higher levels across the efforts described in the previous three spiritually oriented chapters. This alone would be reason enough to take the journey that I've described in this book. But gaining access to self helps us in another way. It raises, and helps begin to answer, the most important question that we humans face: Why am I here?

Recently, the word *purpose* has surfaced a lot in writings by both academics and business practitioners. This trend has been amplified by the collective COVID-19 trauma we've recently experienced, as a result of which so many things that we used to take for granted suddenly came undone. It also seems to have something to do with the most recent generation or two of young people, who enter—or don't enter—the workplace based on their perception of whether a given profession or organization serves a worthy purpose: I want my life to have purpose, and therefore I want to commit myself to something that is purposeful.

I understand and applaud that impulse, but unless properly guided, it may evolve into a prescription for disappointment over the long run. "Purpose" is not something that you put on like a new suit. It's not an external discipline that you embrace. Rather, it's something that comes from within. Its discovery originates when connecting to self.

Why am I here? Gaining access to self clears away much of life's underbrush and turns down the background noise: the spiritual equivalent of putting on noise-canceling headphones. It helps dispel distorted desires that hold you back from reaching your destination. It helps unfulfilled people—even those very successful people who've achieved everything they ever aspired to and are the envy of those around them—leave behind their feelings of restlessness and anxiety and achieve fulfillment. And it opens the door to answering not only the *why am I here?* (the *destination* question)—as I implied above—but also, *where do I want to go next?* (the *journey* question). Both of these questions live deep within us. They shaped and fueled individual and tribal stories in the earliest days of the human species, and they still do today.

## AND THEN, IT DOESN'T STOP

"It's not the destination," Ralph Waldo Emerson once observed. "It's the journey."

As I've said, that's true, as far as it goes. But for many heroes—even most, I'd say—the end of one journey, punctuated by a destination, serves as the beginning of another. Most of my clients achieved their notable career success by being talented, curious, and determined. If their journey with me is successful, they remain all of those things—and now, in addition, they have abundant new reservoirs of energy. They experience more physical pleasure, higher levels of self-confidence, clearer thinking, more love for and from the ones closest to them, and more *truth* in their lives.

So are they going to be content to sit back and simply enjoy the view from the corner office? Unlikely! When I look at Figure 2, what jumps out at me is the *circularity* of Joseph Campbell's metaphor. Is that little hero going to plunk down their backpack to sit by the fire contentedly? No. Most likely, a new destination is going to come into view and a new journey will begin. Simply mastering the art of Being is something that few achieve, and it's something truly to be celebrated. On the other hand: the closer you get to that kind of mastery, the better positioned you are to succeed at becoming a humane leader—or whomever you desire to become!

This is not necessarily what my clients want to hear when they finish their first journey. At least on the conscious level, many of them are inclined to take a break, consolidate their gains, and enjoy their new way of being. And—to be fair—they're eager to pick up the reins in a new way and to exercise the kind of humane leadership they've worked so hard to master and which their colleagues and teams now need them to exercise.

And so I wait for the right moment and then I ask the obvious question: "What's next, for you?"

The answer I tend to get back, in so many words, is, "What do you mean, what's next? Can't I just enjoy mastering my energy? Being a humane leader for a while?"

There are usually two parts to my answer, although they're actually two sides of the same coin. First, I say, let's agree that you have a pretty great new superpower: boundless energy through access to self. Well, how are you going to share your good fortune—your treasure? How are you going to discharge your responsibility to share the benefits of your newfound knowledge with your tribe? Are you going to keep doing what you've always done, just faster and better? Or are you going to help others around you grow? Or are you going to reshape the context of your workplace, toward the end of making it humane?

There are no wrong answers, except—of course—*I'm not going to do anything differently*, and honestly, I never hear that. I *do* sometimes hear a concern expressed along the lines of, "Gee, Ricardo, maybe this company is never going to be the humane place I want it to be."

And that provides the segue to the second part of my answer, which continues to involve destination: "Okay, so where do you want to be in ten years?" Again, it's perfectly okay if someone responds by saying, "I want to keep building this company so that it's ever bigger and ever better."

Yes, but, our firm recently did a CEO survey. Fully half of the responding companies had appointed *three or more CEOs* in the decade between 2011 and 2020. And just under 40 percent of those leadership transitions could be categorized as "emergency departures"—sudden resignations, firings, physical collapses, and so on.

I'm confident that my clients and former clients are underrepresented in those numbers. Why? Because taking care of yourself, understanding yourself, tapping into your inner energy, and exercising confident, humane leadership are all excellent ways to stay tall in the saddle and head off so-called emergencies. But even so, as the average tenure of a CEO continues to decline, year by year, it's sensible to ask and answer my two-word question: What's next? You're now in possession of a magnificent new battery—supplying the best energy all-around. What journey are you going to use it on? To arrive at what destination?

Some of my clients talk about one day becoming entrepreneurs, philanthropists, or angel investors. One of my clients thought about my question for a long minute and said, "Well, after my work is done here, whenever that day arrives, I think I'd like to serve as president of my country."

"And have you taken any steps in that direction?"

"No."

"Why not?"

"Well," she confessed, "I never really had the confidence to explore that, at least until now. Now, maybe I do. In fact, I *should*."

"*Absolutely* you should," I responded. Of course, I knew next to nothing about the reality of becoming the president of a country, but achieving that goal obviously would be a long hero's journey, requiring many thousands of small steps over many years. And that brought to my mind the picture of that little hiking hero in Figure 2. And I realized that it was just possible that a new destination was being allowed to take shape in my client's mind, in real time.

## YOURS CAN BE A HERO'S JOURNEY TOO

Maybe it's time for me to confess the obvious: I took my own version of the hero's journey—going from managing your time to mastering your energy, as this book's subtitle has it—many years ago.

For me, it was a long slog, in part because I was mostly walking in the dark and mostly discovering things with my peripheral vision. Some of the brilliant thinkers and sages whom I've quoted in this book—the Barbara Ann Brennans and Bert Hellingers and Dick Schwartzes—were among the pioneers who stepped forward to help me, but I admit that I had a hard time finding them and figuring out exactly what they were trying to tell me. And if one of them now steps forward to tell me I somehow got it wrong, I won't be totally surprised. My excuse, again, is that I was walking in the dark.

It's my sincere hope that if you decide to take a similar journey, this book—and the stories of the great leaders it presents—will light up your path at least a little bit. Collectively, what do those stories tell you? They tell you that *it can be done.* You can choose to work your way in toward your true self and come out the other side renewed, living in peace, leading from self, and fully committed to elevating humanity and creating a better world.

What's holding you back from gaining freedom of choice and becoming the hero of your own story?

I would say, *nothing.* Go for it. Make it your journey too.

With love!

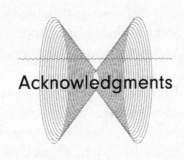

# Acknowledgments

This book is largely about paths within a call to adventure. I want to thank the five groups of allies who supported me on my own path and—by word and deed—helped keep me there.

The first, of course, is my family: my wife, Paty, and our children—Diana, Ricky, and Andy. I'm aware that you figured out what I was talking about long before I did. Thank you for listening and for being patient. Special shout-out to my mom and dad, who were able to bring confidence to their dyslexic son to be able to communicate also in the written word. Who knew, back then, during moments of uncertainty about my future, that I had a book in me?

The second is to my colleagues at Egon Zehnder. I'm especially indebted to Jill Ader, our former chairwoman, whose coherence and inspiration led me to take this call to adventure deeper, and to Ed Camara, our CEO, who believed and supported the launch of this project. As well as to all the colleagues who read and reviewed it; you know who you are. I am deeply grateful for you taking the time in sharing valuable feedback.

Next come the clients that our firm has served over the years. I would never have worked through my ideas in their current form without the benefit of those leaders' strong encouragement, willing suspension of disbelief, justifiable skepticism, and—ultimately—love. Some of their stories appear in these pages. I thank them for their courage and giving me permission to draw on those stories in creating my own.

Fourth, a tip of the hat to the talented people who helped make this book come together. I begin with my developmental editor, Jeff Cruikshank, who with deep reservoirs of patience drew this book out of me. Next, thanks to Jim Levine, my agent, who effortlessly—it seemed—restructured the book and successfully took it to the publishing community. I'm sure that was far harder than it looked, Jim. And to Tim Burgard, Matt Baugher, and the entire team at HarperCollins, thanks for setting high standards and holding us to them. I'm proud of what we've done together.

Finally, I want to thank those intellectual and spiritual guides who put up all those wonderful and indispensable signposts long before I stumbled upon my path and started going down it. Those guides turn up in these pages in roughly the order that I encountered them, learned from them, and became indebted to them.

With deep love and appreciation!

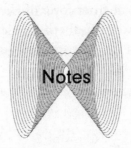

# Notes

## Introduction

1. See the discussion on page 92 of Barbara Ann Brennan's *Light Emerging*. I'll formally introduce Brennan in chapter 1.

2. A PDF of the full report can be found at https://www.egonzehnder .com/cdn/serve/article-pdf/1642761622-6063f84b0988eecb53 297702d589a28b.pdf.

3. Published by HBR Press in 2014, and coauthored by Linda Hill, Greg Brandeau, Emily Truelove, and Kent Lineback.

4. Amy Elizabeth Fox is the CEO and cofounder of Mobius Executive Leadership. For more information on Mobius, please refer to the description on their website at https://www .mobiusleadership.com/about-mobius-executive-leadership/.

## Chapter 1

1. Barbara Ann Brennan, *Light Emerging,* p. 5.

2. See, for example, Darcia F. Narveez's "Dangers of 'Crying It Out'" in the December 2011 issue of *Psychology Today,* online at https://www.psychologytoday.com/us/blog/moral-landscapes /201112/dangers-crying-it-out.

3. This is from the inside front cover of *Hands of Light* (Pleiades, 1987). In that blurb, Elisabeth Kübler-Ross also refers to Brennan as "one of the best spiritual (not psychic) healers in the western hemisphere."

4. From Blake's *The Marriage of Heaven and Hell.*

## Chapter 2

1. After age seven or eight, psychology tells us, we get better at being able to protect ourselves consciously, although loss and illness can still add to our protective emotional layers.

2. See, for example, https://hbr.org/2008/05/overcoming-imposter-syndrome.

## Chapter 3

1. See "Do Schools Kill Creativity?" a TED talk delivered on January 6, 2007, that has since been viewed more than twenty-one million times. Online at https://www.youtube.com/watch?v=iG9CE55wbtY. I felt I had to include the discotheque reference.

2. Refer to Scott's bio at http://scottcoady.com/about-scott.html.

3. *Somatic* is a useful word in my work. It means "relating to the body," especially as distinct from things that relate to the mind.

## Chapter 4

1. "Emile's" is a true story (which combines three different clients to ensure anonymity), except for some identifying details to be kept confidential.

2. I'll credit Barbara Ann Brennan again here for her Human Energy Field (HEF) seven-level framework, on which my own framework is largely based. Readers interested in her version—

which again is aimed largely at the community of healers—should consult chapter 8 of her book *Light Emerging*.

3. From Muir's *The Mountains of California*, Doublebit Press, 2020.

4. Published by New World Library. The book has sold some seven million copies, and its fortieth anniversary edition came out in 2016.

5. See Wim "The Iceman" Hof's website at https://www .wimhofmethod.com/. "Using 'cold, hard nature' as his teacher," his landing page explains, "his extensive training has enabled him to learn to control his breathing, heart rate, and blood circulation and to withstand extreme temperatures. Positively impacting his immune system."

6. See "In Search of Hara," at https://haradevelopment.org/.

7. The parasympathetic nervous system (PNS) is responsible for stimulation of "rest and digest" or "feed and breed" activities that occur when the body is at rest.

## Chapter 5

1. Thank you once again, Emile (anonymous and real), for sharing your story in the spirit of helping others.

2. This last phrase is Barbara Ann Brennan's, from *Light Emerging*, p. 92.

3. See, for example, the Hellinger Institute of DC, online at https:// www.hellingerdc.com/; the Hellinger Institute in Canada online at https://www.hellingerinstitute.com/; and the IFS Institute, online at https://ifs-institute.com/.

4. Again for further details on Mobius Executive Leadership, see their website at https://www.mobiusleadership.com/about -mobius-executive-leadership/.

## Chapter 6

1. The US Navy says that barnacles can increase drag by up to 60 percent, leading to a 40 percent increase in fuel consumption. See the related article on the National Oceanic and Atmospheric Administration's website at https://oceanservice.noaa.gov/facts/barnacles.html.

2. Published by Penguin Books, 2019.

3. This could be the subject of a much longer conversation. But for now, suffice it to say that I think that being dropped at the top of the mountain by helicopter rather than hiking up the mountain makes for a very different view. Also: if you don't hike up, you may not know how to get back down.

4. We'll define "entropy" in this case as a lack of order or predictability.

5. The quote has made its way onto a whole galaxy of inspirational posters, and is also variously attributed to novelist Tom Robbins and cartoonist Berkeley Breathed. I'll stick with the Bandler attribution.

## Chapter 7

1. It takes seventy-five thousand saffron flowers to make a pound of saffron spice. Saffron also has to be harvested manually. It *should* be measured and doled out carefully.

2. I don't have the space here to do this fascinating story justice. Visit the Hellinger website and read for yourself: https://www.hellinger.com/en/family-constellation/.

3. It was the CEO of Mobius, Amy Elizabeth Fox, who introduced me to Ester Martinez. Ester is my Family Constellations teacher. She is one of the best in the world at her craft.

## Chapter 8

1. These facts and figures are from the *USA Today* guide to touring Liberty Island, online at https://traveltips.usatoday.com /walking-up-statue-liberty-62234.html. The article also makes mention of yet another gateway at the statue: the door to the staircase that goes up inside Lady Liberty's arm to her torch. This has been closed to visitors since 1916.

2. Once again, I am grateful to Barbara Ann Brennan's *Light Emerging*, p. 94.

3. See the International Pathwork Foundation website at https:// pathwork.org/about/the-pathwork.

4. This is from Pathwork Guide Lecture 190. The entire lecture is reproduced online at https://pathwork.org/wp-content/uploads /lectures/pdf/E190.PDF. I'll return to Pierrakos in chapter 11.

5. This is Campbell speaking extemporaneously, in response to a question from journalist Bill Moyers. I'll return to Campbell in our epilogue.

## Chapter 9

1. *Light Emerging*, p. 98.

2. The most powerful work in this vein that I've encountered is *Man's Search for Meaning*, by psychiatrist Viktor Frankl—a jewel of a book.

3. This is more evidence of the power of selecting a powerful ally, as Sander was yet another resource first introduced to me by my sage ally Amy Elizabeth Fox.

4. Traditional haiku follows certain rules. See some examples at https://examples.yourdictionary.com/examples-of-haiku-poems .html.

## Chapter 10

1. This is a form of cooperative/argumentative dialogue between individuals, based on asking questions in ways designed to stimulate critical thinking and to draw out ideas and underlying presuppositions.
2. This is something that my wise friend and transformational coach, Mark Thornton, taught me.
3. Again, my thanks to Scott Coady.
4. Of course I'm talking about *leavened* bread here. Unleavened breads get along fine without yeast.
5. Again, my thinking here follows Barbara Ann Brennan's lead in *Light Emerging*, p. 273.
6. One mantra that may help elevate your connection to unconditional love for others (Level 6) is the Ho'oponopono, a Hawaiian mantra. See the Grace and Lightness summary at https://graceandlightness.com/hooponopono-hawaiian-prayer-for-forgiveness/.

## Chapter 11

1. From an interesting essay, "Apocryphal Freud," by Alan C. Elms in *Annual of Psychoanalysis, 2001*, online at https://elms.faculty.ucdavis.edu/wp-content/uploads/sites/98/2014/07/20011Apocryphal-Freud-July-17-2000.pdf.
2. *Creative Visualization*, p. 74.
3. Race tires are designed to last about seventy miles, which—not coincidentally—is about how long a tank of gas lasts. See https://www.indystar.com/story/sports/motor/2016/05/23/s-just-indianapolis-500-tire-much-much-more/84440258/.

## Epilogue

1. Joseph Campbell died in 1987, but a popular TV series that aired in 1988—*The Power of Myth,* hosted by Bill Moyers, and centering on a series of interviews with Campbell—made Campbell's work accessible to viewers around the world.

2. The Executive Breakthrough Program (EBP) is a joint collaboration between Egon Zehnder and Mobius Leadership. Erica Ariel Fox, founding partner of Mobius Leadership, masterfully leads the facilitation of this program.

3. See Yoda raise the ship out of the swamp at https://www.youtube.com/watch?v=E3-CpzZJl8w. As an aside, it was Joseph Campbell himself—in effect, serving in the Old Man's role—who helped George Lucas edit the *Star Wars* script into the final version that moved the world. And if only our lives all had soundtracks by John Williams!

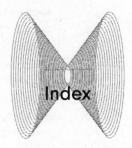

# Index

mind. *See also* clarity of thought
  body, balance with, 52
  body and emotions combined
    with, 39–43
  centering, 32–34
  changing, 105–108
Mobius Executive Leadership, 87
mood, 43
Muir, John, 53
Muir Woods, 159–160
muscle memory
  belief systems and, 102, 106
  Boomerang Effect and, 123
  embodied wisdom, 37
  shaping intentions and, 61
mystery of life, 40, 176, 178–179,
    183, 188

numbing, 56–57, 112

order in family system, 120

pain, emotional
  accepting, 82
  avoiding, 73, 75, 80
  energy blockers and, 7–8
Patil, Dhanurjay "DJ," 26–28
people-pleasing, 15–16
Perfectionist, the, 23
personal interactions. *See* loving
    interactions with family and
    friends
personality, 7–9
physical energy. *See* felt sense
Pierrakos, Eva, 132, 176, 184
pockets of freedom, 47–51
Pollan, Michael, 106–107
power, limits of, 43
presence

accessing self and, 25
body-mind connection and,
    31–32, 104
centering the mind and, 33
creative power from, 123
embodied, 36–37
humane leadership and, 41, 182
in the moment, 56–60, 97, 180,
    192
with those you love, 115
Prodigal Son parable, 120
professionalism
  not showing emotion, 56, 103
  personality and, 9
Protector, 34–35, 175
public speaking, 30–32
purpose
  from within, 193
  collective, 167
  life's, 137–138, 146–151
  "why am I here," 138, 146–147,
    150, 193–194
Purpose Quest ritual, 147–150

reason for being, 180
rigor and caring, balance
    between, 161–163
risk-taking
  belief systems and, 100–102
  self-confidence and, 28, 29
Robinson, Ken, 36
root cause, discovering, 90–91

Schwartz, Richard "Dick" C.,
    34–35, 85, 86–87, 197
seeking the greater universal
    pattern (Level 7), 173–186
  connecting to Levels 5 and 6,
    183–184

About the Author

RICARDO SUNDERLAND is a partner at Egon Zehnder; as a transformational coach, he helps his clients learn how to bring coherence to their leadership, unlock their full potential, and become better versions of themselves.

In addition, he collaborates with the chair and Nominating Committee responsible for CEO and C-suite successions, and supports newly appointed CEOs in their processes of identity transition and role integration.

Prior to joining Egon Zehnder, Ricardo was a partner at KPMG Consulting and a senior vice president at Citigroup. He lives in Marin County, California.

Ricardo earned a BS in finance and marketing from Iberoamericana University and an MBA from IPADE.

One hundred percent of Ricardo's royalties will be donated to charities, including the Egon Zehnder Foundation.